D1236512

1750

PROFILE OF HORACE

PROFILE OF HORACE

D. R. Shackleton Bailey

WITHDRAWN
FROM
UNIVERSITY OF PENNSYLVANIA
LIBRARIES

Harvard University Press
Cambridge, Massachusetts
1982

PA
6411
B28
1982
cop. 3

Copyright © 1982 by D. R. Shackleton Bailey
All rights reserved
Printed in Great Britain

Library of Congress Cataloging in Publication Data

Bailey, D. R. Shackleton (David Roy Shackleton)
  Profile of Horace.
  Includes bibliographical references and index.
  1. Horace—Criticism and interpretation. I. Title.
PA6411.B28   874′.01   82–1010
ISBN 0–674–71325–7   AACR2

WITHDRAWN
FROM
UNIVERSITY OF PENNSYLVANIA
LIBRARIES

UNIVERSITY
OF
PENNSYLVANIA
LIBRARIES

Contents

To
Peterhouse

Preface

'So much has been written about Horace even in the last decade that the mind wearies and sickens' (Gordon Williams, *Horace* (Oxford, 1972)). Some responsibility for this modest accretion must attach to the National Endowment for the Humanities (U.S.A.), which granted me a Fellowship for the year 1980–1981, and to the Master and Fellows of Peterhouse, who elected me a visiting member of their Society and implemented that honour with kindly and generous hospitality. I am further indebted to my Harvard colleague Professor Richard F. Thomas for helpful comments on a first draft.

The following books, other than standard editions of Horace's poems, are referred to by their authors' names:

C. Becker, *Das Spätwerk des Horaz*, Göttingen, 1963.

A. Y. Campbell, *Horace*, London, 1924.

S. Commager, *The Odes of Horace*, New Haven and London, 1962.

E. Courbaud, *Horace. Sa vie et pensée à l'époque des Épîtres*, Paris, 1914.

E. Fraenkel, *Horace*, Oxford, 1957.

A. La Penna, *Orazio e la morale mondana Europea* (in *Orazio* ed. E. Cetrangelo, Florence, 1968).

M. J. McGann, *Studies in Horace's first Book of Epistles* (Collection Latomus, 100), Brussels, 1969.

J. Perret, *Horace*, Paris, 1959.

N. Rudd, *The Satires of Horace*, Cambridge, 1966.

W. Y. S. Sellar, *Horace and the elegiac poets*, Oxford, 1899.

G. Williams, *Tradition and originality in Roman poetry*, Oxford, 1968.

Peterhouse, Cambridge, February, 1981   D. R. S. B.

Biographical Note

Q. HORATIUS FLACCUS was born on 8 December 65 B.C. in or near Venusia in south-east Italy. His father was a freedman, once probably a public slave belonging to the municipality, a business man with a small landed property in the district. Nothing is known of any other relatives. Instead of sending his son to the local school, Horace senior took him to Rome and provided him with the best education available. At about twenty the young Horace went to Athens, the university of the ancient world, and studied philosophy. But his student career was broken off early in 43, when he joined M. Brutus' republican army, receiving the rank of Military Tribune, which was usually held by young men of family and position. Brutus' defeat and death at Philippi in the following year at the hands of Mark Antony and Caesar Octavian ended Horace's military career. He soon returned under an amnesty to Italy, where Caesar Octavian ruled as Triumvir, but his father was dead and his property forfeited to the state. For a livelihood he became a Treasury clerk (*scriba quaestorius*) and also took to writing verses, thus gaining a footing in Roman literary circles. Probably about the middle of 38[1] he was introduced by his fellow-poets Virgil and Varius to Octavian's principal lieutenant in home affairs, Gaius Maecenas, himself a man of letters, and eight months later was invited to join his circle. From that time forward he devoted himself to writing under Maecenas' patronage, living comfortably and uneventfully until 27 November 8 B.C. Maecenas had died only a few months earlier. In later life Horace was on good terms with Maecenas' master, now Emperor Augustus, who at one point invited him to become his private secretary. Horace declined the offer.

[1] See p. 37 n. 13.

Information about Horace's career comes mostly from his works, supplemented by a brief biography (*Vita Horatii*), which seems to be an abridgment taken from Suetonius' *Lives of poets*.

CHAPTER ONE

The Epodes

IN much later life Horace records that after the battle of
Philippi, that is to say after his return to Italy, 'with his
wings clipped' and his paternal property confiscated, he
took to writing verses.[1] Naturally, he will have experimented
with them in his student days at Athens or even before.
Some abortive attempts in Greek, which he mentions in
another place,[2] may belong to those early years. But it was
not until 41, or shortly after, that verse writing became a
serious occupation. 'Enterprising poverty'[3] (*paupertas audax*)
drove him into it, if his own account is to be believed. The
alleged motive would not have disconcerted his contemporaries, who were apt to take a realistic view of such matters.
Hence references in Latin writers to expectant or gratified
heirs, liable to grate on modern sensibility.[4] Or think of
Cicero's second marriage: if a respected elder statesman,
author of edifying tracts, were nowadays to marry a girl
young enough to be his granddaughter, his faithful biogra-
pher would not defend him with the plea that he only did it
to pay his debts with her money.[5] Roman poets, like most
modern ones, could not expect immediate rewards in cash.
But they had benefited from patronage since Rome began to
have a literature, even though the leading poets in the

[1] *Epist.* II.2.49–52.
[2] *Sat.* I.10.31–5.
[3] This does not mean beggary. The clerkship at the Treasury will have been good
for a modest living.
[4] E.g. E. E. Sikes (*Cambridge ancient history* XI, p. 725) found 'glaring want of taste'
in the delightful conclusion of Martial's epigram on the death of little Erotion
(V.37).
[5] Plut. *Cic.* 41.

generation before Horace had not required it. When he came
back to Italy, its ruler's principal minister, Maecenas, was a
versifier himself, interested in promoting poetic talent. Why
should Horace not hope to recommend himself through his
work to Maecenas' literary protégés and through them to the
great man himself? That, after all, is what happened. Status
and financial ease duly followed.

Horace's earliest extant verse is in two genres: iambics (the
Epodes) and satires, modelled respectively more or less upon
the eighth-century Greek Archilochus of Paros and the
second-century Roman Lucilius. In the former area he
claimed to be a pioneer:

I was the first to show Parian iambics to Latium. I followed the
rhythms and spirit of Archilochus, but not the matter and the
words that hounded Lycambes.[6]

By 'spirit' he meant primarily the invective for which Archilochus was famous, though perhaps including his vigorous
handling of other themes, love or politics. Seeing that
Lucilius too was regarded first and foremost as a satirist in
the modern sense, attacking contemporaries whom he dis-
liked or reprobated, some have been tempted to relate
Horace's literary choices to the unsatisfactory state of his
own fortunes at the time, picturing him as an angry young
man, or as he would rather have put it, a snarling dog; and
certainly those few of his extant poems which can be plausibly
dated to this period are conspicuously lacking in characteristic Horatian good humour. But whatever his inclinations
may have been, he was no Archilochus or Lucilius. Not for
him 'the matter and the words that hounded Lycambes'—
by which he seems to mean, not just that his epodes were not
actual translations, but that they did not lampoon individuals, at least not under their real names, however closely
otherwise some of them might follow Archilochian precedent.

The classic example is Epode 10, in which the direst
maritime mishaps are imprecated upon 'stinking Mevius',
who was about to set out on a voyage. A papyrus fragment

[6] *Epist.* 1.19.23–5.

discovered in 1899 revealed that Archilochus wrote just such a poem. But whereas Archilochus' target is described in the fragment as a one-time friend who had injured the poet and betrayed him, this Mevius is a lay figure, whose personality and offence (apart from the epithet) nowhere emerge in the twenty-four lines of Horace's poem. Fraenkel[7] was surely right to contend that a poetaster of that name mentioned by Virgil is irrelevant, since Horace's poem, which was written for posterity, has nothing to suggest him but the name, which posterity was unlikely to remember. But Fraenkel's contrast between the conditions of poetry-making in *c.* seventh-century Greece and first-century Rome, however true and instructive, is rather beside the point. Lucilius, and later Catullus and Calvus, had lampooned their enemies, who were sometimes people of consequence, as savagely as Archilochus. But they were men of standing and property, allied to powerful figures in a republican community. The son of an ex-slave, living on sufferance under the autocracy of the man against whom he had fought at Philippi, was in no position to follow their example. His targets had to be either persons unidentified if not imaginary or persons unlikely to retaliate. The latter choice would have put Horace on the level of the cowardly dog he chastises in Epode 6, hostile to harmless strangers but chary of tackling wolves. In the Satires, it is true, both categories are admitted, but only in passing allusions; whereas the iambic tradition called for sustained onslaughts, like Epodes 8 and 12, 'as unpleasant reading as anything in ancient literature'.[8] Both purport to address women with whom Horace has had sexual relations

[7] Pp. 26f., laying it down that 'no external material can, in the case of a real poem, that is to say of a self-contained poem, supply a clue not contained in the poem itself'. By 'external material' Fraenkel obviously meant material which readers, contemporary and later, could not fairly be expected to know about. I may add a remark made à propos of Martial (*Cl. phil.* 73 (1978), 287): 'In interpreting this poet it is a sound rule never to assume explanatory facts which are not in the poem or fairly to be inferred. He wrote to be understood by posterity, and although he sometimes overestimated posterity's intelligence, he did not expect it to be clairvoyant.' But this does not preclude allusions *not* important to the understanding of the poem, as that to Trebatius Testa's habits in *Sat.* II.1.7–9 (see Rudd, *Phoenix* 18 (1964), 230f.). Little would be lost if we did not happen to know from Cicero of Trebatius' addiction to wine and swimming.

[8] Sellar, p. 120.

but whom he now rejects. The first is rich, old, and unspeak-
ably ugly. The second (unless they are one and the same) is
likewise old, but her principal handicap is one she shared
with Mevius. Unlike her predecessor, however, she is let
speak for herself and even achieve a certain grisly pathos
(21–4):

For whom were woollen threads, double-died in Tyrian purple, so
rapidly a weaving? Why, for you, so that when you dined among
your friends none should have a more loving lady.

Why did Horace some ten years later, having created the
amiable persona which was to delight posterity, publish
these unsavoury reminders of a manner he had discarded?
Probably because they stood firmly in the iambic tradition.[9]
He will have looked upon them as displays of technique and
expected readers to do likewise. Such is the Mevius Epode,
so meticulously analysed by Fraenkel. Such almost, but perhaps not quite, is Epode 6, in which a literary bully is
menaced with Archilochian vengeance, an anticipation of
Satires II.1.39–56. Here as there the easily-perceived empti-
ness of the threats makes them amusing. Was that Horace's
intention and have we here a first faint foretaste of the
self-mocker who appeals so adroitly to our sympathies
later on?

Archilochus may well have provided a prototype for
Epode 4, another invective. Its object, an upstart ex-slave, is
introduced as an inveterate enemy, but the only reason for
thinking he existed is the last line, *hoc, hoc tribuno militum*;
surely an allusion to Horace's own army rank and the
carping tongues it sharpened.[10] The distinction between ex-
slave and freedman's son touched Horace in a highly sensitive spot.[11] If the piece was about a real Tribune, it has
more point. However, we cannot be sure.

To all seeming, these five poems exist wholly or almost
wholly in and for themselves, with no significant relationship
(unless it be in Epode 4) to persons or experience. Probably

[9] Plutarch (*De curios.* 10) writes of Archilochus' 'unseemly and licentious' attacks
on women.
[10] See p. 19.
[11] See G. Highet, '*Libertino patre natus*' (*Am. journ. phil.* 94 (1973), 268–81).

the same holds for the three Canidia pieces (Epode 5, Satires 1.8, Epode 17)—'un jeu littéraire', as Lejay called them. Canidia and her sister-sorceresses are classable with Mevius, except that the principal witch is allowed a few conventional characteristics demanded by the theme. The second and third members of the trilogy are clearly and successfully comic, but in the first the comic is wedded to the macabre in a manner which has been aptly compared with the *Ingoldsby Legends*; an interesting experiment which does not quite come off. The child-sacrifice's sufferings and blood-chilling threat of posthumous vengeance (elaborated in one of M. R. James' best ghost stories) are altogether too powerful to fit in acceptably with the scene of Sagana bust-ling about 'with spiky hair bristling like a hedgehog or a running boar' or the farcical situation between Canidia and her elderly lover, whose infidelities are the object of the gruesome exercise.

The Canidia series has been thought suggestive of a Hellenistic inspiration, and there is no knowing whether Archilochus left anything to give rise to Epode 2, *beatus ille*.[12] After sixty-six lines in praise of country life, the reader is brought up short with the revelation that he has not been listening to Horace but to 'money-lender Alfius' *(faenerator Alfius)*, who having made up his mind to put his money into land promptly changed it. Alfius existed. About a century later a saying is attributed to the same 'moneylender Alfius' in Columella's treatise on agriculture.[13] The identical desig-nation suggests that even in Horace's time it may have crystallised in usage, like Thomas the Rhymer, or Trader Horn, or the fictional Parson Adams, or the presumably mythical Farmer Giles. If so, Alfius was probably in his grave. The poem's four-line coda was compared by Alfred Noyes[14] to the mocking conclusion of the first Epistle: the Wise Man is every thing the Stoics say, except when he catches cold. There the purpose is clear, to lighten the fore-going moralities with a touch of irreverent wit; but Alfius'

---

[12] Though see Fraenkel, pp. 59f.
[13] I.7.2.
[14] *Horace: a portrait* (1947), pp. 123f.

function is harder to diagnose. Is the main part of the poem
a skit on fashionable Arcadianism? Or is Horace compensat-
ing an exposure of his deepest feelings with an ironic
flippancy? Both interpretations have had their advocates.
An answer must depend on one's assessment of the sixty-six
lines. To me this itemisation of rural joys and ploys in jog-
trot metre conveys no feeling at all.[15] But its banality is not
manifestly enough contrived to be satirical. Rather this
epode is another exercise on a theme, only for once Horace
warns us against making it into anything more. Part of the
joke is the intimation that the speaker, who in 61 would seem
to be on the farm, is actually still in Rome (73).

It is a reasonable guess that the closer to Archilochus an
epode appears, the earlier its putative date. Of those already
noticed, most or possibly all may have come between 41 and
38 or 37, when Horace joined Maecenas' circle. Epode 3,
addressed to his patron, is equally a 'jeu littéraire', but of a
novel type. It exploits an alleged personal experience in
terms of parody. Horace had eaten garlic and suffered an
upset stomach. Through eighteen lines he rails against the
offending root with an assemblage of references to Canidia
and to mythological poisonings—'a good deal of mocking
pathos and quasi-Archilochean indignation delivered with
feigned grandiloquence.'[16] The parody[17] is the *raison d'être*,
not the incident itself, which may just as well be real as
imaginary. The last four lines seem to have caused a mis-
understanding:

But if ever again you desire such a thing, my gamesome Mae-
caenas, I pray your girl-friend may put her hand up when you try
to kiss her and sleep on the edge of the bed.

[15] Cf. D. O. Ross, *Am. journ. phil.* 100 (1979), 244: 'The almost dream-like
succession of rustic delights (clichés all), strung out with such naive simplicity, was
hardly intended to represent any compelling reality.'   [16] Fraenkel, p. 68.

[17] Applied to ancient literature the term 'parody' has almost always one of two
meanings: (a) mocking imitation of a genre (e.g. the mock-epic *Battle of frogs and
mice*), including use of an elevated style for a down-to-earth or comic theme, and
(b) a piece modelled for comic effect on another piece, like *Catalepton* 10. Ancient
examples of a third form, in which a writer's idiosyncrasies are 'taken off', as in Max
Beerbohm's mischievous masterpiece *A Christmas garland*, would not be easy to find,
apart from particular expressions (cf. Rudd, pp. 109f.) and the famous scene in
Aristophanes' *Frogs*.

Commentators often infer that Horace ate the garlic at Maecenas' house as the victim of a practical joke on his host's part.[18] But 'if ever again you desire such a thing' is not to say 'if ever again you do such a thing'. Presumably Maecenas too ate the garlic. As for the epithet 'gamesome' (*iocose*), it is probably only a by-product of the amatory context. Compare *Priapea* 83.24f., a poem attributed to Tibullus: *puella nec iocosa te levi manu/fovebit apprimetve lucidum femur*. Indeed it is quite likely that Markland's conjecture *iocosa*, applying to the girl, is what Horace wrote.

The three love-epodes, 11, 14 (also addressed to Maecenas), and 15 likewise seem written for the writing's sake, though the excuse in 14 for failure to complete the promised Book of Epodes could be real and the opening of 15 strikes an arrestingly romantic note. Affinities with contemporary love-elegy are easily sensed, but Horace's fancies are represented as fleeting—no *Cynthia finis erit* for him. Not that the elegists too are without their less constant moments.

The characteristic which most of the epodes have in common, their autonomy—the poet's experience, factual, emotional, or intellectual, apparently counting for little—is not shared by the remaining five. The two national epodes, 7 and 16, usually dated 38–36, are immediately relevant to the ongoing civil wars, whether or not Archilochus had provided antecedents. To deny them some emotional impetus would be bigotry, even if they do not ring entirely true. As remarked by a Scottish dominie in 1857, the notion that Rome's calamities were in expiation of Remus' murder by Romulus 'might be regarded as far-fetched'. True, Virgil in his *Georgics* (1.501f.) attributes them to an even remoter guilt. But what is tolerable in Virgil as an *obiter dictum*, is harder to accept as a climax, portentously prefaced. In Epode 16 'it is easy to see that the complete unreality of the constitutional conditions under which Horace's assembly appears to transact its business is in harmony with the complete unreality of

---

[18] The objection (see Giarratano) that there is no word for 'again' in the Latin can be countered with Ov. *Trist.* 1.8.23f. *denique lugubres vultus numquamque videndos/ cernere supremo dum licuitque die* and Stat. *Theb.* 9.212 *numquam tibi dulce superbi/regis onus*.

the poet's proposal'.[19] The Islands of the Blest in context with the grim realities of the period are at best a pleasing whimsy.

No such criticism applies to the acknowledged gem of the collection, Epode 13, the only one with a philosophical message. It is a well-integrated poem, harbinger of the Odes and prototype of Housman's 'The chestnut casts his flambeaux'.

Shortly before publishing the series in 30, Horace added the two 'Actium' epodes, 1 and 9, both addressed to Maecenas. Housman's demonstration[20] in 1882 that Epode 9 was (or purports to have been) composed just *before* the news of Octavian's victory has often been ignored, for example by Fraenkel,[21] who held that since 'the idea of a letter to Maecenas is wholly out of place' the poem 'purports to be the idealised rendering of some part of a conversation' at a banquet, perhaps in Horace's house. Why not a soliloquy such as is often addressed to an absent person (e.g. Odes III.29)? Housman's thesis was adopted by E. Wistrand in his monograph on the poem,[22] though he went back to Buecheler's theory that Horace wrote it on board ship at Actium. His acknowledgements of Housman's priority[23] were so far from explicit that one of his reviewers[24] remarked: 'Like Giarratano, Wistrand maintains that the dramatic date of the poem is prior to Actium'; whereas Giarratano, whose commentary on the Epodes was published in 1930, names G. Friedrich as originating the theory in his book *Q. Horatius Flaccus*, published in 1895 (Friedrich too had agreed with Buecheler). No word of its real author, Housman.[25]

Horace seems to have started writing his iambics with close attention to his ancient model, but as time went on he experimented more freely. The result, apart from the common denominator of metre, is heterogeneous like no other

[19] Fraenkel, p. 46.
[20] *Journ. phil.* 10 (1882), 193–6 = *Classical papers*, pp. 6–8.
[21] Pp. 71–5.
[22] *Horace's ninth Epode* (1958).
[23] Pp. 25n., 30.
[24] R. T. Bruère in *Cl. phil.* 55 (1960), 142.
[25] Nor yet in Williams, pp. 212–19.

collection in classical literature, not only in topics but in tone and essence.[26] Two prominent features of his other work are missing. There is practically no moralising, and though most of the poems are in the first person they carry little of his personality, to say nothing of deliberate self-projection.[27] For that he used a more appropriate medium.

---

[26] 'The book of Epodes is rather a jumble' (Campbell, p. 135).

[27] The self-descriptions in *Epod.* 12.3, 'a delicate young man with a sensitive nose', and 1.16, 'unwarlike and rather delicate', do not take us far.

CHAPTER TWO

The First Book of Satires

(i) *The second Satire*

CONCURRENTLY with the Epodes Horace wrote his two Books of Satires, or 'Talks' (*sermones*) as he also called them, poems of miscellaneous content, generally ranging from about 80 to 150 hexameters.[1] Satire-writing had been the life work of his acknowledged model Lucilius. Although not the inventor of the genre (as Horace at one point calls him),[2] it was Lucilius who made the hexameter its standard metre and whose vitriolic attacks on contemporaries gave the word 'satire' its modern meaning—originally it meant 'medley'. The fragments of his thirty Books are so meagre that the extent and nature of Horace's debt to him, as to Archilochus, is pretty much a matter of speculation, of which there has been enough and to spare. One leading feature of Lucilius' work, which he probably inherited from the real inventor of satire, Ennius, was the lavish interjection of the author's personality and day-to-day affairs, stressed by Horace in a memorable passage:[3]

He used to confide his secrets to his books as to trusted friends, running to them and no one else if aught went wrong and likewise if aught went well. And so it is that the old gentleman's whole life lies open, as in a picture on a temple wall. Him I follow.

Horace was to exploit this traditional element in his own way. But Satire 2, the only one which can confidently be assigned to his earliest period before his acceptance by Maecenas, is objective, like the Epodes. As to its date:

---

[1] The two short Satires 7 and 8 of Book I and the long Satire 3 of Book II are exceptional.   [2] *Sat.* 1.10.48.   [3] *Sat.* II.1.30–4.

The bawdy theme and treatment, the plentiful and aggressive use of names, and the absence of any reference to Maecenas all point to an early date. So does the rather uncertain structure.[4]

No one can miss the contrast in tone between this and the two post-Maecenatian pieces on either side of it, though all three can be classified as moral discourses ('diatribes') and are roughly similar in design. But the uncertainty of structure in Satire 2 which troubles modern readers may be an illusion. In the middle section, as printed in our editions, ill-related and contradictory ideas seem to bob up like jacks-in-boxes, but perhaps this is because editors leave out some crucial quotation-marks. Suppose that what Horace intended here is not a monologue but two dialogues.

The first thirty lines are plain sailing. For the first time (chronologically) Horace puts forward his favourite doctrine of the Golden Mean. Sinners and fools go to extremes in their anxiety to avoid the opposite extremes. They become spendthrifts so as not to be misers, fops so as not to be hobbledehoys, and vice versa. Finally, to introduce the main topic, the pursuer of married women (*matronae*) is set against the frequenter of the 'stinking brothel':

> *sunt qui nolint tetigisse nisi illas*
> *quarum subsuta talos tegat instita veste:*
> *contra alius nullam nisi olenti in fornice stantem.*　　30
> *quidam notus homo cum exiret fornice, 'macte*
> *virtute esto' inquit sententia dia Catonis.*
> *'nam simul ac venas inflavit taetra libido,*
> *huc iuvenes aequum est descendere, non alienas*
> *permolere uxores.'*　　35

Some there are who don't care to touch any woman except one whose ankles are covered by the matron's robe. Another, on the other hand, wants none but the girl who stands in the stinking brothel. As a man he knew was coming out of a brothel, 'Bravo!' says the divine verdict of Cato. 'For when foul lust blows up the veins, this is the place for young men to go, instead of interfering with other people's wives.'

---

[4] Rudd, p. 10.

Why should *Horace* quote Cato in defence of brothel-going, one of the two objectionable extremes? And the two and a half lines of justification are rather what might be said to an opponent than what Cato would say to the young man in the story. This is told by a scholiast (Horace has left out the second and most important part):

As Cato was passing by, a man came out of a brothel. He made off, but Cato called him back and congratulated him. Later, when he noticed the man coming out of the same establishment rather often, he said: 'Young man, I praised you for coming here from time to time, not for living here.'

Do not lines 31–5 belong to an imaginary interlocutor (*alius* of 30), who after quoting Cato adds his own comment?

> '*quidam notus homo cum exiret fornice, "macte*
> *virtute esto" inquit sententia dia Catonis.*
> *nam simul ac venas inflavit taetra libido,*
> *huc iuvenes aequum est descendere, non alienas*
> *permolere uxores.*'

Horace makes no reply in detail; the 'stinking brothel' condemns itself.[5] 'Cupiennius, who likes married ladies, would not agree' is all the answer he vouchsafes. Then comes the turn of the opposite extremists, Cupiennius and his like. In lines 37–46 Horace lists some of the unpleasant things that could happen to an adulterer caught in the act. It is so much safer, he concludes, to traffic with freedwomen:

> *tutior at quanto merx est in classe secunda,*
> *libertinarum dico, Sallustius in quas*
> *non minus insanit quam qui moechatur!*

But how much safer is trafficking in the second class, freedwomen I mean, about whom Sallustius is as crazy as an adulterer!

Horace's word *merx*, 'traffic', offers an opening to a second interlocutor—let us call him Cupiennius—, the advocate of the opposite extreme (adultery). *Sallustius . . . moechatur?* is

---

[5] For his own part Horace admits more than once to philandering, but nobody could truthfully accuse him of 'bad haunts' (*Sat.* 1.6.68).

his retort: 'If it is money you are talking about, freedwomen can be as ruinous as "matrons". Look at Sallustius.' He puts it in the form of an ironical question:

> *'Sallustius in quas*
> *non minus insanit quam qui moechatur?'*

So in Plautus' *Epidicus* (699f.) one speaker rebuts another by tacking on a relative clause, as a question, to what the latter has said:

> *aio. vel da pignus ni ea sit filia.*

Yes. Or lay me a wager that she is not his daughter.

> *quam negat novisse mater?*

When her mother says she doesn't know her?

Horace comes back (in summary; 49–53):

True, but Sallustius should have kept the expenses on his affairs down to reasonable limits. Then neither his reputation nor his pocket would have taken any harm.

Cupiennius rejoins (in summary; 53–63):

Ah, but all he cared about was to be able to say 'I never touched a married woman', and that makes no defence for squandering money and good name. Wrongdoing is wrong, whether a married woman is involved or a slave-girl.

The point is valid as far as it goes, and Horace does not contest it. Instead he reverts to what he has said already, that adultery involves physical risk, whereas a gowned slave-girl (*ancilla togata*; but *togatae* also include free single women 'of easy virtue' and freedwomen) is safe. Besides, the 'gowned girl' can be thoroughly inspected beforehand. From line 64 onwards the sequence presents no problems.

After line 36 the doctrine of the Mean has fallen into the background. It turns out to have been only a duct into the main stream, the disadvantages of adultery and the advantages of satisfying sexual need where it can be done safely and easily. But there is no contradiction. The other extreme, the 'stinking brothel', is still to be avoided. All else is intermediate and so to be recommended. Within this middle

range Horace's argument does not distinguish one category
from another, as some of his interpreters have supposed.
Neither does he take account of widows, divorcees, or un-
married but respectable girls. In Roman society respectable
young women normally *were* married from a very early age,
however often they might change their husbands.

(ii) *A personal statement (Satire 6)*

Horace's first Book of Satires was published in 35, the second
some five years later, about the same time as the Epodes. The
individual poems, along with others not included in the
published Books, will have had many readers or auditors
before they reached the public at large. But publication was
a major step. Why did the Satires (the first Book) take
priority? One would think that by 35 Horace had composed,
or could have composed, enough Epodes to make a Book.
Perhaps Maecenas and his literary friends preferred the
Satires. But it may be relevant that in them Horace presented
himself as well as his work. The Epodes would not have
done that.

As already noticed, and as Horace went out of his way to
point out,[6] autobiographical personalia belonged to the tradition of the genre as inherited from Lucilius. But if Lucilius
confided his life to his verses with all its incidental ups and
downs, his successor operated very differently.[7] No ego-
centric chat or artless self-unburdening, but a studied self-
presentation by means of more or less seemingly casual
self-reference backed by a pervading ethos. Sellar[8] rejoiced
in Horace's 'frank trust in himself and in his reader, and the
self-respect with which he admits the world into his confidence'. After all, there was something to be said for the
fundamentalism which accepted the author on his own terms,
as indeed there was something to be said for living in the late
nineteenth century; but we do not live in it. Alternatively,
the Horatian self-portrait can be appreciated independently

---

[6] See p. 10.   [7] Cf. La Penna, p. vii.   [8] P. 4.

of any presumed likeness to the original. 'The main point,' writes W. S. Anderson,[9]

is that Horace produced a Socratic satirist probably quite un-representative of himself; and this satirist, the speaker in his *Sermones*, is one of the greatest achievements of Horatian poetry.

But the autobiographical personalia of the first Book of Satires turn so largely upon the newly established connexion with Maecenas as to allow the conjecture that a pragmatic concern to set that momentous development in a sympathetic light had more than a little to do with the matter.

Horace's career, like that of an otherwise dissimilar artist, Richard Wagner, was turned around once and for all by the acquisition of a great patron. Suetonius says: *primo Maecenati, mox Augusto insinuatus*. According to Fraenkel,[10] Suetonius 'puts on the facts his own interpretation, the interpretation of a man living at the court of Hadrian'. The implication that patron-hunters behaved much otherwise at the court of Hadrian than at other times and places seems precarious. But Fraenkel misunderstood Suetonius, in whose usage *insinuatus (est)* means merely 'was introduced into favour'.[11] But when he goes on:

That need not worry us since for the history of Horace's friendship with Maecenas . . . we are provided with the most reliable and detailed evidence,

Mephistopheles whispers: 'Horace's evidence.' At any rate we can assume that Horace's tactics, if he had to employ tactics, were more subtle than those of his 'bore' in Satire 9. His introduction to the great man is immortalised in the sixth (52–62):

I could not say it was by a lucky chance that I won you for a friend. No accident, to be sure, brought me in your way. Virgil, best of beings, and Varius after him told you about me. When I met you

---

[9] In *Critical essays in Roman literature* (ed. J. P. Sullivan, 1963), p. 17.

[10] Pp. 15f.

[11] So in *De grammaticis* 21.2 of the grammarian Melissus: *quare cito manumissus, Augusto etiam insinuatus est*, also in later Latin, as the *Augustan History* (XVIII.21.8 *quis quo esset insinuante promotus*).

face to face, I blurted out a few words—shyness had my tongue, stopped me saying more. I did not tell you that my father had been a famous man or that I rode around a country estate on a thorough-bred, but simply what I was. You, as your habit is, say only a few words in reply. I take my leave. Eight months later you call me back and bid me join your circle.

Only that? Maecenas had presumably been already in-formed of Horace's background and current circumstances. Something must have been said on literary matters. Obvi-ously Maecenas had been shown specimens of Horace's work, so unlike what was to come. Did the 'few words' in-clude something like this?

'Young man, your friends tell me you have talent and these things of yours I have been reading prove it. But the flavour is rather pungent for my taste. These descriptions of hideous old hags now—quite in the style of Archilochus, no doubt, or perhaps I should say Hipponax, but not *precisely* the kind of thing *we* want. When you write your next contri-bution, I wonder whether you could not contrive something a *soupçon* more *urbane*? Possibly you might recall some amusing incident, say something that happened in your army days. Or what about a "Defence of satire"? But of course you will decide for yourself. Just let me see what you do and perhaps we shall be meeting again.'

From the date of the second summons Horace was a made man. Perret's[12] theory that he was drawn to Lucilius by his desire to write about himself, is discountenanced by the im-personal character of the second Satire. Rather, as suggested above, that desire, so prominent in the first Book of Satires, may have been induced, or at least stimulated, by his estab-lishment with Maecenas. The notoriety and envy excited by his new position among literary rivals are easily imagined, and others too will have looked sourly on this ex-republican upstart, as he was seen more and more often in company with the second most powerful man in Italy. The sixth Satire, written perhaps two or three years later, is a personal apologia designed to disarm ill-will.

Like the master of camouflage he is, Horace begins on a

12 Pp. 75-7.

note of defiance. For all his exalted birth Maecenas (so the Satire starts) does not look down as most people do on unknowns like Horace, a freedman's son. The elaboration of Maecenas' aristocratic ancestry in the first four lines shows 'a magnificence far above the average level of a *sermo*',[13] even though the Etruscan forbears are not called kings, as in later apostrophes, but only 'commanders of great legions'. Irony lurks. Maecenas too was a parvenu from the traditional Roman standpoint, a 'foreigner' like Cicero, who had usurped the power, if not the dignity, of Rome's historic families.[14] He evidently enjoyed references to his lineage and will have appreciated the subtle dig at Roman prejudice. But that is by the way.

Maecenas, the poem goes on, maintained that provided a man was born free (a highly sensitive point with Horace)[15] it did not matter who his parents were. He knew that long before Servius Tullius[16] became King of Rome, men of humble origin had risen high; whereas the aristocratic Valerius Laevinus[17] was despised and rejected by the voters, in spite of their usual foolish partiality for noble birth. If the common people showed so much good sense, what ought men like Maecenas[18] to do, far, far removed from the vulgar herd?

So far, then, a commonplace in any class-conscious society: *nobilitas sola est atque unica virtus*, 'a man's a man for a' that'. Sellar's notion (not peculiar to him) that 'Horace, in this vindication of himself, announced a great change in social opinion, which the empire, as the great leveller of ranks, introduced',[19] is moonshine. When the grandee Appius

[13] Fraenkel, p. 101.

[14] R. A. Schröder in *Wege zu Horaz* (ed. H. Oppermann, 1972), p. 38, takes the view that Maecenas was too proud to become a Senator, which would be further cause for aristocratic or even bourgeois resentment.

[15] See p. 4 n. 11.   [16] Actually slave-born.

[17] Perhaps taken out of Lucilius. This branch of the great Valerian clan vanishes from ken in the first half of the second century B.C.

[18] *Quid oportet/vos facere a vulgo longe longeque remotos?* *Vos* is Bentley's conjecture for the vulgate *nos*. If the latter is retained, I would take the repetition *longe longeque* as ironical ('we, who are, of course, so far . . .'), the irony being naturally against Horace himself, not Maecenas. But this seems over-complex.

[19] P. 59.

Claudius told Cicero in effect that he ought to have more respect for his betters, Cicero wrote in reply:[20]

I conceived myself to have become the equal (never the superior) of you and your peers . . . If you think otherwise, you will do well to pay rather close attention to what Athenodorus son of Sandon has to say on these matters, in order to gain a better understanding of the meaning of *eugeneia* (good birth).[21]

Horace for his part knew that Bion of Borysthenes, whose influence on his Satires he later acknowledges,[22] had flaunted his low beginnings.[23]

But Horace's object was to placate, and this was not the way. Camouflage apart, he owed it to his self-respect to make the obvious play, but at the point when a typically conservative-minded Roman reader might be imagined as getting restive, Horace lets him see that it was only a feint and that he is really the most modest of mankind, fully acceptant of his social limitations. A new section begins with line 19:

Well, so be it.[24] The people would *rather* vote for a Laevinus [though in fact they had not done that] than for a [plebeian] Decius, and Censor Appius would have struck me off the senatorial roll if my father was not freeborn.

What is coming next? More on the same tack? Instead, a sudden *volte-face*:

It would have served me right, actually, for not keeping in my place.

After which, a passage (24–44), stuffed with examples, against the folly and impropriety of political climbing (never mind now what happened before King Tullus).

Horace knew that sympathy is not won by argument:

Now I come back to myself, the freedman's son, yes, the freedman's son they all carp at. Nowadays they do it because I am close to

---

[20] *Ad fam.* III.7.5.

[21] He might have cited Euripides, frag. 52, 53 (Nauck) and other passages quoted in Stobaeus 29 (86).

[22] *Epist.* II.2.60.   [23] Diog. Laert. IV.46.

[24] *namque esto*. I think *namque* should be translated 'well' or 'why', not 'for'.

you, Maecenas; in time gone by it was because I commanded a Roman legion.

This, for Horace, uniquely bitter outburst prepares the ground for the most 'pathetic' passage in his works, outside the Odes. First, however, a few well-chosen words on the friendship (49–64). The Military Tribunate, for a freed-man's son, *was* invidious (disarming admission), but not so Maecenas' friendship, which is given only to the deserving—no nasty jockeying for favour (*prava ambitione procul*; we think of Satire 9).[25] The account of the introduction follows next, with its delineation of a young man almost too shy to make the most modest of self-presentations.

I think it a grand thing to have pleased so discriminating a judge of moral worth, not because I have a distinguished father but because my life and hands are clean (62–4).

And if Horace is a good, nice person (fairly nice, anyway; has his faults, of course), liked by his friends, as he apologetically admits to be the case: 'my father is the cause.' Then follows the filial tribute which has perhaps done more than anything else he wrote to win the liking and respect of his readers, down to its memorable conclusion: 'never in my right mind could I wish to have had a better father.'

Classical writers prefer not to end on a climax. By a subtle transition we are taken back to a theme already adumbrated. Horace has no ambition to be a figure in public life, he is content with a modest existence which allows him to observe the city doings around him, to read and write (the reminder that he is, after all, a noted man of letters slips into place in the least assuming of imaginable ways), take his exercise in Mars' Field and his ease at home.

I walk on my own where my fancy takes me. I ask the price of vegetables and flour. Often of an evening I wander through the tricky Circus and the Forum. I pause at the fortune-tellers. Thence I take myself back home to a plate of leeks, pulse, and pancakes. Three slaves put on the dinner. On top of a white marble slab stand two jugs and a wine-cup, and beside them a cheap cruet, an oil-flask and saucer—Campanian ware. Then I go to sleep, with

[25] See pp. 20–2.

no concern about having to get up early in the morning . . . I lie
till ten o'clock, then go for a stroll or I read or write something
pleasant to muse on, after which I use some oil—not the kind that
dirty Natta steals from the lamps. But when I am tired and the sun
waxes strong, reminding me of bath-time, good-bye to the Field
and my game of ball. After a not too hearty lunch, just enough to
save me from spending the day on an empty stomach, I take my
ease indoors. Such is the life of folk who stand clear of ambition's
griefs and burdens. Such are my consolations.[26] I shall have a more
pleasant time of it thus than if my grandfather and father and
paternal uncle had been Quaestors every one.

A beguiling curriculum. But Maecenas' *convictor* did not
always sit (or rather lie) down to a solitary dinner at home.

So in the sixth Satire Horace tactfully and adroitly handles
a delicate theme. As a bid for the approval of literate Rome
it could hardly be bettered, but as an autobiographical document it raises questions. Anyhow, if carpers went on carping
it would not be Horace's fault. Maecenas must have been
delighted with the piece, and its merits will not have been
lost upon Maecenas' master Caesar, himself no fumbler in
the arts of propaganda.

(iii) *Satires 9, 3, 5 and 1*

While Horace's personality is much in evidence in his
perennially amusing encounter with the 'bore' (Satire 9), it
is secondary to the bold and sly device in virtue of which he
lends support to his frontal defence against the carping
world in Satire 6. Were they saying that he had wormed his
way into favour by making overtures to sundry of the great
man's friends or hangers-on? None other than Horace will
illustrate by a neat transposition of roles how such things are
done and what a mistake it would be to suspect him of doing
them. The 'bore', who is really a vulgar place-hunter, accosts

---

[26] 'Horace cannot refrain from that sarcastic *consolor*—a word which betrays that
his wounds were still smarting' (Rudd, p. 48). Is it not rather a gentle touch of
irony? Some people might feel deprived in such a way of life, not Horace. As Rudd
observes elsewhere (p. 252), he uses virtually the same word in a similar context in
Sat. II.6.117.

him in the street, as he walks along deep in his own thoughts, introduces himself as a poet in the still modish 'neoteric' style (*docti sumus*), and successfully resists Horace's polite but increasingly desperate efforts to shake him off. The heart of the business is reached in line 22; when the 'bore' gets to what is really on his mind:

'If I know myself, you will find me as valuable a friend as Viscus or Varius. Who can turn out more verses than I, or faster? Who is a nimbler dancer? Why, my singing makes Hermogenes jealous.'

Horace manages to get a word in edgeways: Does the 'bore' have a mother or family to care about his welfare? The answer is a brisk negative: 'Buried the lot.' That prevents Horace from following up his question. What he had intended to say the reader is left to guess without too much in the way of a clue—a most unusual trick for a writer to play. Perhaps it is a calculated stroke of realism; such things do, after all, happen in conversations. Guesses have been plentiful. One, that a physical threat is implied, can be eliminated because, as Rudd says,[27] Horace is on the defensive throughout. Besides, the function of mother and relatives would be to advise or restrain.[28] But, as Rudd also says, the purpose of the question ought to be to get rid of the 'bore'. Might not Horace have continued! 'Then let them tell you to steer clear of *satirists*'? 'He is a mad bull, give him a wide berth.'[29]

His attempt to get away from the 'bore's' subject is in vain. Back it comes in 43–8:

How do you get on with Maecenas? There's one who picks and chooses, knows what he's about. Nobody has used good luck to better purpose. Now you would have a great back-up, somebody to play second fiddle, if you cared to introduce yours truly. Damme if you wouldn't push right to the head of the queue!'

The 'bore' has revealed himself as everything that Horace is not and most dislikes. Carpers, take note. His answer is austere, not to say priggish (48–52):

---

[27] P. 284 n. 41.
[28] Cf. *Sat.* II.3.57–9 *clamet amica/mater, honesta soror cum cognatis, pater, uxor:/'hic fossa est ingens, hic rupes maxima! serva!'*   [29] *Sat.* 1.4.34.

'We don't live there in the way you suppose. There is no cleaner house, none further removed from such unpleasantness. It never stands in my way if somebody has more or knows more than I do. Everyone has his allotted place.'

Carpers, having base minds, will be incredulous; let them hear themselves in the 'bore': 'That's a hard one to swallow.' 'Nevertheless, so it is.'

The 'bore' is not crushed. He will bribe servants, lie in wait for Maecenas in the street, never give up; Rome was not built in a day. But at this point the dialogue is interrupted by the arrival of a third party. No more is said of Maecenas, or needed saying.

*

Horace's account (Satire 5) of a journey taken probably in the spring of 37 (very soon after he had joined the circle)[30] in the company of Maecenas, who was travelling to Brundisium with a party of friends on an important diplomatic mission, produced a broadside from A. Y. Campbell:[31]

Considering the occasion, and still more the persons . . . it would, one would think, have been impossible to write an account that should be for posterity quite uninteresting. But Horace has surely come as near to that as he or anybody could.

The interest of contemporaries will have largely been directed to the challenged comparison with Lucilius' account of a journey to Sicily. But posterity in general has been less critical than Campbell, finding the versified travelogue adequately entertaining, even though Maecenas and high politics are kept well in the background and the adventures of the road are rather small beer. Horace's role is presented as purely social, and he makes as little of that as he well could. Enough that he was one of the party. Stressed, on the other hand, is the warmth of his friendships with fellow-members of the circle. Joy at the advent of Plotius, Varius and Virgil, sorrow at Varius' departure touch with emotion

---

[30] See p. 37 n. 13.   [31] P. 166.

an otherwise pedestrian narrative. By contrast, an erotic frustration is recorded in baldly realistic terms, embarrassing to later admirers but presumably acceptable to contemporaries, both as a touch of nature and as an echo of Lucilius.

*

Friendship is one of the two main subjects of the third Satire, a moral discourse like the second, but in later, kindlier vein. The failings of a friend, at least lesser ones, are to be treated with indulgence. As in the other two moral discourses in Book I, the approach is indirect. Tigellius the Sardinian, a favourite with the Dictator Caesar and later with Caesar Octavian, whose death made the starting-point of Satire 2, is portrayed through nearly twenty verses as a type of inconsistent behaviour. Then (19f.):

Now somebody might say to me: 'What about yourself? Have *you* no faults?' Indeed I have, different and perhaps—less serious'.[32]

Immediately after this we are introduced to one Maenius, who criticises another nonentity called Novius behind his back. This leads into the first main theme.

There seems to be some mismanagement. The sequence is clear enough.[33] What Horace has been doing to Tigellius, Maenius does, and is blamed for doing, to Novius. There are indeed some crucial differences. Tigellius is dead, Novius presumably alive. Tigellius was no friend of Horace's as Novius is of Maenius—that is implied in what follows, though not stated specifically. And Horace is a satirist, whose recognised business it is to ridicule or lambast those who deserve it. That the parallel between Horace and Maenius is only superficial is evident on reflection; but at first sight Horace does appear to be convicting himself of an 'un-

---

[32] *et fortasse minora.* Perhaps *haud* (edd. vett.) ought to be read for *et*. Otherwise *minora* is a joke, παρὰ προσδοκίαν. The reader expects 'greater ones'.

[33] Contrary to Rudd's statement (p. 5), I do not think Fraenkel meant to deny *any* connexion.

sympathetic' misdemeanour, something he never does elsewhere for all his self-depreciation.

The two principal themes, that 'a friend should bear a
friend's infirmities' and that (as against the Stoics) some
wrongdoings deserve lighter punishment than others, are
both 'sympathetic'.[34] The first person singular crops up more
than once, but most notably in lines 63–6, in which the last
of several examples goes to show that not only are we harsh
to our friends' faults but even give disagreeable names to
their virtues:

> *simplicior quis et est, qualem me saepe libenter*
> *obtulerim tibi, Maecenas, ut forte legentem*
> *aut tacitum impellat quovis sermone molestus :*   65
> *'communi sensu plane caret' inquimus.*

Suppose again somebody is rather guileless, so that he interrupts
a friend as he is reading or just not talking with some tiresome
chatter, as I should often be fain to thrust myself on you, Maecenas:
we say he is quite lacking in social sense.

qualem . . . obtulerim is usually taken to mean 'as I myself have
often readily [or 'without ceremony', 'ungeniert'][35] put myself in your way'.[36] As just remarked, Horace's self-depreciation has its limits. He is not by way of letting himself appear
odious or contemptible. Following the standard interpretation we have to believe that in his anxiety both to allude to
and to play down his privileged position vis-à-vis Maecenas
his good taste deserted him. But the standard interpretation
is solidly based on mistranslation.[37] The proper rendering of
me libenter obtulerim is demonstrable from Cicero: *quin etiam
corpus libenter obtulerim* (*Philippics* II.118) means 'I should even
be glad to put my body in the way', not 'I have even been
glad . . .' So Horace is writing, not of something he has
often done, but of something he would often like to do (being

---

[34] 'The most humane of all the diatribes' (Rudd, p. 9).

[35] 'Schütz takes *libenter*="without ceremony" . . . a meaning which I doubt
whether *libenter* can bear' (Palmer). I too.

[36] Differently, but still wrongly, Wickham: ' "I should never mind having shown
myself . . ." Some editors in criticising this passage have credited Horace with less
than his usual irony.' Palmer's note, however, comes close to the mark.

[37] That much was noticed by E. C. Woodcock, *Cl. rev.* 52 (1938), 9.

'rather guileless', a 'sympathetic' trait), if he had not too much 'social sense' to make a nuisance of himself—in fact, he is having it both ways. It is one of those seemingly casual touches which go to make up the image, as well as a reminder of his close, if deferential, association with the great man.[38]

*

Although the first Satire, and so the whole Book, is addressed (i.e. dedicated) to Maecenas, it is almost as impersonal as the second—Horace is modestly slow to introduce himself—except, an important exception, that it exemplifies a new ethos, encapsuled in a well-known phrase: 'What forbids us to tell the truth with a smile?'

(iv) *A satirist's defence (Satires 4 and 10)*

The fourth Satire contains a quotation from the second (line 92). That is one clue to its date. Another is the absence of Maecenas' name, which in this Book it shares only with the second and two others, both short, unimportant, and un-datable, the seventh and eighth. Moreover, it seems to have been written before Horace thought of publishing his work (71f.). On the other hand, it is unmistakably in his later manner. Hence my speculative suggestion that it may belong to the waiting period which followed his first meeting with Maecenas. As his literary apologia it is complemented by the personal apologia, Satire 6. The two were given places of honour in the centre of the Book, separated by the innocuous Journey to Brundisium. At the same time the defence of satire is placed appropriately after (though very likely written before) the discourse on fault-finding between friends in Satire 3. This defence is on two fronts, literary and ethical. The former predominates in the first sixty-five lines, but of

---

[38] Cf. Fraenkel, p. 88: 'No attentive reader can miss the note of gratitude and happiness that permeates this brief personal digression. The passage looks like a first tentative step on the road that was soon to lead the poet to perfect mastery in describing his own way of life, his βίος.'(!)

the piece as a whole Fraenkel[39] remarks that 'of the two aspects under which Horace attempts to vindicate his *satura* it is the moral, and not the artistic, aspect which is given the lion's share'. Does not that indicate, given Horace's devious ways, that the artistic aspect interested him more?[40] At least it is certain, for his whole work attests it, that he was a self-conscious artist, profoundly concerned with his art.

He makes two points. First, as to Lucilius: contrary to the normal practice of ancient writers and of Horace himself in relation to his Greek prototypes, he is frankly critical of the father of satire (as a satirist Ennius did not count). He grants Lucilius humour and a keen eye for moral obliquity; but what clumsy, slipshod stuff! Lucilius' trouble was that he used to turn out two hundred verses in an hour standing on one leg and thought it a marvellous achievement. He shirked the labour that writing demands—good writing, that is to say. Unnecessary to add to this indictment (which he brings elsewhere against early Latin poetry as a whole)[41] that its author was just the opposite. The importance of meticulous workmanship and tireless revision remained the first article in Horace's literary creed through thirty years of writing. And Lucilius' surviving fragments bear out his strictures, none more than the longest of them, eleven doggerel lines on the meaning of *virtus*.[42]

His other point is that the Satires are not to be regarded as poetry but as metrical prose; presumably a plea against the application of false canons of judgment, unless it be merely Horatian self-deprecation. Not that this stops Horace from referring to himself as a poet, in playful disregard of pedantic consistency, and even making the word (*poeta*) stand for the special category of satirists.

On the moral side the defence concentrates on the characteristic which Lucilius had introduced and made paramount, attacks on named individuals. Satire 4 begins with the start-

---

[39] P. 127.

[40] 'It is characteristic of an εἴρων to say less about the more important achievement' (McGann, p. 83).

[41] *Sat* 1.10.67, *Epist.* 11.1.64–75, *A.p.* 258–62.

[42] Marx 1326–36. They have been mistranslated in the past, e.g. by Warmington and Rudd (p. 99), but Krenkel gets them right.

ling assertion that Lucilius derives entirely from Aristophanes and the other poets of the Athenian Old Comedy, saving only that he used different metres. Plainly an exaggeration, which the reader must cut down to proper size: Lucilius attacked contemporary malefactors as Aristophanes and the rest had done.[43] A similar *modus operandi* on Horace's part can be observed in Satire 1.80–3, lines addressed to an imaginary miser:

But if you are suffering from an attack of influenza or if some other mischance has confined you to your bed, do you have somebody to sit beside you, prepare the poultices, ask the doctor to put you on your feet and give you back to your children and loved ones?

Of course he has! The miser is rich, and when rich curmudgeons fall ill they are not left unattended. Even the families do not always avoid the sickroom. Presumably Horace has in mind that such mercenary attentions only make the invalid more comfortable physically and do nothing for his sense of inner abandonment. But that is not what he says. Instead, he makes a statement (it amounts to that) plain contrary to experience and common sense, and the reader has to make the best of it.

The case is somewhat different in Epistles 1.1.76–82, where Horace is explaining why he is not prepared to take his moral judgments ready-made:

You [the Roman people] are a many-headed monster. What am I to follow, or whom? Part of the people are eager to farm the public revenues, some with pastries and fruit hunt greedy widows or catch old men to put in their private zoos. Many make money in secret by usury. However, granted that different men are attracted by different aims and pursuits: can these same people stay an hour with the same object in view?

The fact that there is more than one way of making money is irrelevant. What Horace ought to have said is that some go after money, others after power, others after pleasure, and

---

[43] After Rudd's definitive refutation (p. 91) there is no need to dispute the notion that Horace in this satire sets himself up as a satirist with a missionary purpose against a merely destructive Lucilius. It is to be reiterated that he does not here claim to have such a purpose (see La Penna, pp. xlviif.).

so on (compare the sixth Epistle). The temptation to put in some lively descriptive writing on different ways of getting rich was too much for him. Satirists can be reckless and one-sided, like Juvenal, but in Horace's case it might be more appropriate to think in terms of an occasional (though rare) truancy from realities, a sort of poetic license. As a final instance take Odes III.16.21–4:

The more each man denies himself, the more he will get from the gods. Stripped bare, I seek the camp of the undesirous. I cannot wait to become a deserter from the ranks of the rich.

Horace was not a rich man and, if we are to take his word for it, did not want to be one. And despite his talk of leaving everything behind (*nil cupientium/nudus castra peto*) he had no idea of abandoning his Sabine farm and becoming a Diogenes. Lines 37f. of the same ode make that clear:

However, I do not live in grinding poverty, and if I wanted more, you [Maecenas] would not refuse to give.

He is in the toils of an inappropriate metaphor: 'To satisfy it completely, Horace must have been a rich man who gave up [rather 'wanted to give up'] his wealth. All he really means is, that he would choose a modest competence in preference to great wealth' (Wickham). But a modest competence is what he already has. The urge to change sides is an illusion.

   To return to the fourth Satire: it is not impossible that some of the plentiful personal allusions in the early Satires, represented for us only by the second, had caused offence. The targets, no doubt, were insignificant, when not dead or fictitious, but even the insignificant have feelings and friends. However, Horace shows no uneasiness about possible retaliation. So far as it can be taken seriously, his defence is a vindication of his own good nature, as Rudd's summary[44] well brings out:

In justifying his satire against the charge of malice Horace makes the following points: Old Comedy and Lucilius branded criminals (1–7); unlike Crispinus I write very little (17–18); unlike Fannius I do not seek publicity (21–3); the innocent have nothing to fear

[44] Pp. 89f.

(67–8); I do not intend my poems to be sold, nor do I give public
recitations (71–4); real malice is something quite different—it
means backbiting one's friends and spreading scandal (81–103); I
was taught to notice wicked behaviour by my father; he used
individuals simply as examples of different vices (103–31); I am
really quite a good-humoured fellow (91–2, 103–4); my observations are for my own improvement (137–8); and my writings are
just an amusing pastime (138–9). He then concludes the piece with
a disarming smile (140–3).

The arguments do not amount to much. Horace's butts
are mostly social liabilities ('Rupilius smells of comfits,
Gargonius of goat') rather than criminals. Victims would
hardly be appeased by being told that he wrote little and
that little for private circulation; if he had been in earnest
with this plea, would he have left it in the published edition?[45]
As for Horace's father, who brought him up to see moral
warnings in flesh-and-blood examples, *his* lessons were given
in private. The real strength of the rebuttal lies in the non-
chalant good humour with which these flimsy justifications
are deployed. But I do not get the impression that either
Horace or his contemporary readers were seriously exercised
on this score, apart from a few nobodies whom he may have
offended.

The tenth Satire, an appendix to the fourth, was ostensibly added shortly before the Book was published. Horace's
outspoken criticism of Lucilius had raised some eyebrows.
He does not withdraw it,[46] though he now admits that
Lucilius was *comis et urbanus* (hardly more than *facetus* in the

---

[45] 'The Augustan poets—and, probably, other poets in other ages—when they
published a book did not trouble to bring every detail in it "up to date" or to
eliminate from it everything that had been appropriate at the time of writing but
proved less appropriate at the moment of publication' (Fraenkel, p. 287, in another
connexion). A good observation, but hardly covering the destruction of a case
which the poet had been genuinely anxious to make.

[46] On the other hand, I cannot go all the way with Rudd (p. 94): 'Horace therefore stands by his criticisms of Lucilius' style, but modifies what he said about his
tone. While granting that Lucilius was witty, he now maintains that his wit was too
often harsh and vulgar. This is a less favourable estimate than that given in 1.4 . . .'.
Actually, Horace says nothing about vulgarity; his reference to Laberius' mimes
clearly relates to their uncouth style. When he says that humour is usually more
effective than harshness (14f.), a criticism is no doubt implied, but one need not
make too much of it. Everyone knew that Lucilius was *acer in satura*.

fourth) and less unpolished than might have been expected[47]
or than were the generality of early Latin poets; and he dis-
claims any attempt to strip the champion of his title, as it
were—as the inventor of the genre Lucilius was the greater
man (48–55). But he also takes occasion to formulate his own
prescriptions for this kind of writing and names a number of
contemporaries, including his companions of the Journey,
Plotius, Varius, Maecenas and Virgil (in that order), whom
he writes to please. Set against this élite are the vulgar herd
and certain objectionables whose literary affiliations are
indicated in lines 17–19:

Pretty Hermogenes never read them [the poets of Attic Old
Comedy], nor that monkey whose sole accomplishment[48] is to
chant Calvus and Catullus.

Further allusions to Hermogenes and his friends ('louse
Pantilius', 'silly Fannius') show them as Horace's detractors,
while lines 17–19 in their context imply that they were involved in the controversy about Lucilius. But these people
were 'neoterics' in the still ongoing Alexandrian trend. As
remarked by Cicero,[49] the 'neoterics' did not think much of
Ennius, or presumably of early Latin poetry in general. Why
should people who had no time for anything written much
over thirty years ago (for the 'monkey' will have been more
or less representative) be up in arms about Horace's strictures upon an early poet? Surely not because of any special
affinities with Lucilius.[50] But neither were they simply using
him as a convenient stick with which to beat Horace. Some
manuscripts begin this satire with eight verses which certainly do not belong to it and in all probability do not belong
to Horace:

Lucilius, I am going to demonstrate how full of faults you are on
the evidence of your defender Cato, who is preparing to emend
your bad verses . . .

[47] That is the only possible sense of the controverted lines 65f.: *fuerit limatior idem/
quam rudis et Graecis intacti carminis auctor (rude et Graecis intactum carmen = satura).*

[48] *Doctus* has 'neoteric' associations.

[49] *Tusc.* III.45.

[50] As contended by Rudd (pp. 119–23).

In his satire Horace demonstrates nothing of the kind, but the information is credible, whatever its source. Valerius Cato was coryphaeus to the contemporary 'neoteric' group,[51] but he was also a teacher of literature (*grammaticus*). It is therefore not surprising to find him employed in editing (as 'Horace's' unkind words seem to imply) an early writer. It appears that he produced a defence of Lucilius against the attack in Satire 4, and naturally his friends and disciples would chime in. They did not have to know or care about Lucilius in order to sneer at Horace's presumption.

To have closed the collection with so personal a piece as Satire 9 might have seemed in doubtful taste. The tenth, while harking back to the fourth is comparatively objective.[52]

---

[51] On this now contentious subject see R. G. M. Nisbet, *Journ. Rom. stud.* 69 (1979), 147.

[52] So at least it seems to me despite Rudd's question (p. 153): 'Why should 1.10 . . . be so sharply personal in tone?'

CHAPTER THREE

The Second Book of Satires

THE tenth Satire of Book I takes up again the 'artistic aspect' of the fourth; the 'moral aspect' is resumed in the introductory satire of Book II. However, there is hardly a pretence any longer of serious vindication. Its opening statement, that some people think Horace's satire too bitter while others find it 'nerveless', lets an important cat out of the bag. As polemic, the first Book *is* undeniably tame and Horace knew that the second was going to be even tamer. Against that criticism he had no defence, except that the times and his own place in them did not allow of his 'scouring the town' as Lucilius had done. To offer it would provoke an embarrassing question: why pretend to write satire at all? The real answer is that as a Lucilian satirist Horace is not in genuine business; he only keeps up the personal digs and scoffs as a concession to the convention of the form. But that was something he did not care to admit directly, so he makes belief that it is only the opposite criticism of excessive bitterness (probably a figment of his own) that calls for a reply. This reply is cast in the form of a consultation with the eminent jurist Trebatius Testa, once a friend and correspondent of Cicero, now in late middle age, whose dry responses are part of the comedy.

Having explained that he has to write because he cannot sleep at night and again that he comes from Venusia, a town of fighters, Horace unexpectedly engages to attack nobody unprovoked (39–46):

But this pen shall attack no living person without provocation. It shall protect me like a sword snug in its scabbard. Why should I make to draw it, if I am safe from hostile bandits? O Jupiter, Father and King, grant that the weapon lie by and rust away nor

let any man harm my peace-loving self! But whoso stirs me up
(*garde à qui me touche*, I cry), he shall rue the day. All Rome shall
bruit his name notorious.

Burlesque, of course, but with a serious implication. Since
Horace is obviously not in earnest with his polemics, complaints that they lack bite will be beside the mark.

   Every animal defends itself with its natural weapons. The
wolf uses his teeth, the bull his horns. Not to labour the point,

whether a quiet old age awaits me or death's black wings hover
over me, whether rich or poor, in Rome or (should chance so order
it) in exile, whatever my life's style, I shall write (57–60).

Not 'write satire' but simply 'write'. The ambiguity is convenient.

   Keeping up the masquerade, Trebatius warns that 'a
friend' (obviously meaning Maecenas) may not be pleased.
'Not at all,' answers Horace. Scipio Africanus the younger
and his friend Laelius did not object to Lucilius' onslaughts
on the highest in the land and the general public to boot.
But the logical corollary, that as a satirist he, Horace, could
likewise rely on Maecenas' approval and support, is nimbly
side-stepped. Instead, an unblushing irrelevance: 'Envy herself will reluctantly admit that I have associated with the
great'—the consciousness of circumambient envy (*invidia*)
accompanied Horace throughout his career. After some
more persiflage the piece ends with a peal of laughter:
solventur risu tabulae.

   Whoever expected Lucilian vitriol after all this jollity
would have his own blockishness to blame for his disappoint-
ment. 'In this poem we are struck again and again with a
playfulness amounting to farce' (Rudd).[1] Even a topic not
ordinarily suited to levity, gets an amusing twist or two.
Trebatius advises his client that if he positively has to write,
he had better sing the deeds of victorious Caesar—that
would be work well rewarded. 'No,' says Horace, making the
most lighthearted 'refusal' (*recusatio*) in Augustan poetry
(12–15),

---

[1] P. 129.

I wish I could, good papa, but I lack the strength. Not everyone has it in him to describe battle-lines bristling with Roman javelins and Gauls perishing with their spears broken or the wounded Parthian sliding from his steed.

The epic magniloquence of this is pointed by the prosaic fact that the future Augustus had fought no campaign against either of Rome's two most fearsome foreign enemies. Well then, what about a panegyric on Caesar's noble character? That suggestion receives Horace's qualified assent (17–20):

I shall not miss the opportunity when the opportunity comes. Only at the propitious time will Flaccus' words pass through Caesar's attentive ear. Stroke him the wrong way and he will kick out in all directions.

That Horace could allow himself such freedoms says much for the security of his position at the end of the thirties. No harm in letting the world see that. Naturally the passage had been 'cleared' with Maecenas, and, whether through him or directly, with Caesar, who could already be cited as an admirer of Horace's work (84). Caesar, for certain, was amused.

*

The two personal narratives in the first collection of satires have no counterparts in the second. Extended narrative (unless the fable of the two mice in II.6 be reckoned as such) is found only in the farcical dinner-party of II.8, with satirical and gastronomic overtones and probable Lucilian antecedents. Horace's decision to write no more 'Journeys' or 'Encounters' is much to be deplored, for in the latter at least he gave us something delightful and unique in ancient literature, as we have it. Surely contemporaries were appreciative. Or were they? The 'Journey' bore the stamp of Lucilian ancestry. Did the 'Encounter', a very different product, seem to them just an oddity?[2] Did Horace himself, having written it with a particular self-protective purpose,

---

[2] The supposed Lucilian origin of the 'bore' was exploded by Housman; cf. Rudd, *Phoenix* 15 (1961), 90–6.

lack the enterprise and imagination to exploit a vein which he had only struck by accident?

Literary discussion too is absent from the second Book, apart from its flippant introduction. Horace was to return to that in his closing period. Evidently he had said all he wanted to say for the time being.

Offsetting these subtractions, much attention is paid to a new topic: food. The fourth of the eight satires of Book II is a gastronomic lecture, miscellaneous, mock-serious, and dry, put into the mouth of one Catius, who professes to be re-tailing it from an authoritative but anonymous source. Food and wine are prominent in two others, the second (a sermon on plain living) and the eighth. Perhaps Horace's interest in this subject was an effect of prosperity and gourmet company. Culinary verse was nothing new. The Horatian specimens are as tedious as Horace ever lets himself become, also am-bivalent. For he makes it none too clear whether he is tilting at gastronomy or merely at the pomposity which is apt to go with it. The poet who as good as accuses himself of gluttony in II.7 can hardly have intended Farmer Ofellus' austerities in II.2 to be taken as his own *letzter Ernst*.

The staple diet in this Book, however, is ethical. Horace is often supposed to have been deeply interested in moral philosophy. His ideas on the subject are neither original nor profound nor wide-ranging; but for a writer without a great deal to say and with a rare capacity for saying it, this was an attractive topic, demanding little of intellect or imagination, but capable of lively illustration and readily lending itself to the Horatian blend of ironic humour, worldly tolerance and down-to-earth good sense. Two of his main guidelines are laid down in the first Satire of Book I: the folly of greed and the Golden Mean. Without questioning his inner assent to both, it is possible to agree with those who discount the urge to reform his fellow men with which he has often been credited (or saddled).[3] A third doctrine comes more to the fore in his later work,[4] the *adiaphoria* of the Stoics, indifference

---

[3] 'Barton Holyday, a seventeenth-century critic, protested that "a perpetual grin, like that of Horace, doth rather anger than amend a man". Much he would have cared!' (L. P. Wilkinson, *Horace and his lyric poetry* (1945), p. 104).

[4] First mooted in *Sat.*II.7.83–88.

to externals. That involved some conflict between aspiration and attainment.[5]

Book II avoids *ex cathedra* homilies like the first three satires of Book I. Monotony lay that way (averted to some extent in Book I by the amorality and indecency of Satire 2) and possible reader-resistance. In II.2 the preacher is thinly disguised by ascribing the sermon to a philosophically-minded peasant. II.5, on the other hand, is an arresting novelty, a dialogue in the Underworld between Ulysses and his mentor Tiresias. Uniquely for Horace, it concerns a particular social malpractice (touting for legacies), and its mordant humour has reminded many readers of Juvenal. Was it intended to demonstrate what this satirist might have achieved along other lines?[6] The portentously lengthy third and the seventh are dialogues between Horace and another, who like Catius does the preaching at second or third hand.

Self-portrayal persists, but the style and emphasis have shifted. Horace no longer had to introduce himself or to deprecate hostility. The apologetic newcomer has given way to a comfortably self-assured personage, whose detractors will bite on granite, forced to admit that he has been the companion of great men.[7]

*

Throughout most of his literary career Horace wrote poems ostensibly relating to incidents and situations in his daily life. On the reality and importance of this factual background his interpreters are perennially divided. Satire II.6 stands alone as quite indubitably a veritable reaction to a major personal event, Maecenas' gift of a modest but still substantial property in the Sabine hills, where Horace could spend his summers, or part of them, undisturbed, away from

---

[5] See La Penna, pp. li–liii.

[6] 'Had Horace followed this track still farther, he might have been in danger of changing from the pugnacious yet good-natured *Venusinus* into a venomous *Aquinas*' (Fraenkel, p. 145).

[7] *Sat.* II.1.74–8.

'the smoke and opulence and noise of wealthy Rome'.[8] It begins with a prayer, 'magnificent without being heavy' (Fraenkel), that plainly comes from the heart, but Horace has not forgotten his sense of humour: 'Make fat the squire's livestock and everything else except his head.'[9] Where poets and such are concerned, the word *ingenium* (translated 'head') connotes 'talent', the talent of which Horace had been careful to say almost nothing in his earlier personal confession.[10] Thence he passes on to Maecenas and the trials of life in the big city, with a picture of himself hurrying through its crowded streets (28–62):

I must needs struggle with the crowd, do violence to slowcoaches. 'What's with you, lunatic? What's got your feet so angry?[11] Are you supposed to knock everybody out of your way when you run back to Maecenas with your mind on your appointment?' I like that, music in my ears, I won't say otherwise. But so soon as I arrive at the gloomy[12] Esquiline, other people's affairs come leaping up by the score, through my head, all round me. 'Roscius begs you to join him in court at eight tomorrow morning.' 'Quintus, the Clerks beg you not to forget to come back today—a very important matter has cropped up.' 'Please see that Maecenas signs these papers.' If one says 'I'll see what I can do', he insists: 'Oh, you can if you want'.

Seven years will soon have flitted by—it's nearer seven than six[13]—since Maecenas first took me into his circle, merely as someone to take in his carriage on a journey, a confidant for little secrets such as 'What's the time?' or 'Is Gallina the Thracian a match for Syrus?' or 'The mornings are beginning to nip, we must take care'—anything safely entrusted to a porous ear. Through all

---

[8] *Odes* III.29.12. Winter visits will probably have been only occasional, though *Sat.* II.3 finds him at the farm during the Saturnalia and the Soracte ode (1.9) is located there (see D. West, *Reading Horace* (1967), pp. 3–6).

[9] The joke in this form is Horace's, though, as Professor Thomas has pointed out to me, it is an adaptation of Callimachus, *Aetia* I.fr.1.23f. (cf. Virg. *Ecl.* VI.4f.).

[10] See p. 19.   [11] See p. 84.

[12] Maecenas' palace on the Esquiline Hill was built on what had been a cemetery.

[13] This is, I think, the only legitimate sense of line 40, *septimus octavo propior iam fugerit annus*. It cannot mean 'seven years have now passed, indeed almost eight.' If *Sat.* II.6 was written in the winter of 31–30, as the allusions in lines 53–6 are held to indicate, Horace's first introduction to Maecenas must have taken place not much earlier than the middle of 38.

this time, every day, every hour, jealousy of our old friend Horace
grows and grows. Have the two of them watched the games together, played ball together in the Field? 'There's a lucky man,'
say they all. If a nasty rumour comes seeping down from the Forum
through the squares, whoever meets me consults me: 'Well, my
dear chap, *you* must know, you are in close touch with Olympus—
have you heard anything about the Dacians?' 'Why no, nothing.'
'Ah, you will have your joke.' 'No, may all the gods confound me
if I have heard a thing.' 'Well then, has Caesar promised farms in
Sicily to the ex-service men or is he going to give them out of
Italian land?' When I swear I know nothing about it, they are
lost in wonderment at my discretion and take me for the closest
mouth in creation. So the day goes to waste, alas, but not without
a prayer: 'Oh, when shall I see the country again? When shall I
be free to enjoy myself, forgetting this life of cares, with books of
ancient authors or with sleep and idle hours?'

Horace is a well-known figure these days, Maecenas' recognised intimate, a source of information and favours. His
modest disclaimer convinces nobody. In fact, he is boasting,
but skilful camouflage and self-deprecatory humour remove
all offence. This flattering persecution in Rome is presented
as a foil to the ensuing tableau of Horace in his new country
home, his patron's gift, affably entertaining rustic neigh-
bours at a simple meal, while the slave-children receive
tit-bits from his friendly hand. The talk runs on standard
problems of ethics, enlivened by edifying tales, like the tale
the town and country mice, than which Horace never contrived a more felicitous finale.

*

The third and seventh Satires of Book II exploit a variation
of self-commendatory technique. In Book I Horace's good
points had been persuasively intimated: the solider virtues,
seconded by warm affections, modesty, good breeding, and
a sense of humour. Failings were admitted (not very serious),
but not particularised. A man of tact does not enlarge upon
his faults in company which has not yet learned to appreciate
him. Satire 3 of Book II begins and ends with a self-indict-
ment, in the form of a dressing-down by Horace's partner in

the dialogue, one Damasippus,[14] a former art-connoisseur and dealer who had overbought himself into bankruptcy, turned Stoic, and was now generally supposed to be crazy. He opens the conversation by chiding Horace for his laziness —the poet does nothing but drink and sleep, neglecting his work, except for an occasional revision of something already written. Note the recurrence of Envy (13):

Are you trying to placate Envy by ceasing to do good work?[15]

By implication Horace's work is important, the serious business of his life, which makes him an effective (and envied) member of society. Contrast Satire 1.6.

The preliminaries lead into a lecture lasting some three hundred lines to inculcate the Stoic paradox that all fools, i.e. all mankind except the Stoic Sage, are mad. Horace hears this out with exemplary patience, then asks what particular folly, i.e. madness, does he, Horace, suffer from. First, replies the Stoic, he apes the 'life-style' of his superiors, building,[16] for example, as though he was Maecenas, which he is so very far from being—like the frog in the fable who tried to inflate herself to calf-size. Then (321–6):

'Now add poetising, which is to say, add oil to fire; if any man who does that is sane, sane you will be. I say nothing of your shocking temper.'
  'That's enough.'
  'Your style of living which you can't afford.'
  'Mind your own business, Damasippus.'
  'Your passions for a thousand girls, for a thousand boys.'
  'O greater madman, spare the lesser!'

To take these charges seriatim (leaving out the stock joke about mad poets): (1) Laziness. Not too 'unsympathetic' a trait; and the publication of three Books of poems allowed the reader to make his own appraisal. (2) Building (aping

---

[14] Not a fictitious character, though perhaps no longer alive. His full name was probably L. (?) Licinius Crassus Damasippus, of noble birth and the son of a republican Senator killed in 46. See my paper in *Am. journ. anc. hist.* 3 (1977), 162f. also *Two studies in Roman nomenclature* (1976), 46f.

[15] *Virtute relicta. Virtute* means roughly 'energy' or 'effectiveness'. Not, as Rudd, 'by deserting the cause of virtue'.

[16] Probably at the Sabine villa.

his betters). Horace is saying: 'I realise that my head may
look swollen, but this very admission shows that it is not.'
(3) Hot temper. The thumb-nail sketch of himself in Epistles
1.20 includes the item: 'irritable, but easily appeased.' That
was a 'good' fault.[17] Cicero writes to Atticus about his
irascible brother Quintus:[18]

I don't need to tell you, for you already know, what a kindly,
aimiable fellow he is, how impressionable both in taking offence
and in laying it aside.

And later in the same letter:

If you take the view that the best people are apt to be easily provoked and also easily appeased, that this mobility, so to speak, and
impressionability of temper is usually the sign of a good heart . . .
then everything, I hope, will be easily assuaged.

(4) Living beyond his means. Obviously venial. (5) Philandering. Readers would recall an incident on the highway
to Brundisium and smile.
    Qui s'accuse, s'excuse.

*

Satire II.3 seems to have been so well received in Horace's
circle that he was encouraged[19] to produce another piece on
the same lines (he even links the two by the detail that both
dialogues are supposed to take place during the Saturnalia),
but in Satire II.7 the self-incrimination is more venturesome.
The speaker, with occasional interlocutions from Horace, is
his slave Davus, doubtless an imaginary creation—the name
is as stock as ' 'Arry' once was for a cockney—who takes
advantage of traditional Saturnalian licence to tell his master
home truths. The first item on this new charge-sheet is inconsistency, not so much of behaviour (as with Tigellius in

---

[17] See Fraenkel, p. 361. He was mistaken in attributing the idea to Aristotle
(*Eth. Nic.* IV.11.8, 1126a), who merely says that irascible men get angry with the
wrong parties and for the wrong reasons and in excess, but quickly drop their
anger, 'which is their best trait'.

[18] *Ad Att.* 1.17.2, 4.

[19] Or so I would suppose, in preference to the common opinion that Horace's
powers of invention were exhausted.

I.3) as between profession and practice. Better to be firm in bad courses, says Davus, than unstable.[20] Horace poses as an admirer of the good old times, but would not live in them if he could. He wants to be in the country when he is in Rome and vice versa. He pretends to enjoy a simple meal at home, but an eleventh-hour invitation from Maecenas sets him in a flurry of excitement. Thus prepared comes another Stoic paradox, that all but the Wise Man are slaves (Davus has picked it up from the doorman of Crispinus, the Stoic preacher at whom Horace had taken more than one barbed shot in Book I). But the discourse is mainly about Horace's alleged indulgence in fleshly pleasures. Twenty-six lines (46–71) takes him to task for chasing a married woman. With its (for Horace at this stage) unparalleled patch of obscenity and its references to the physical risks of adultery, the passage takes us back to Satires I.2. Another specimen of inconsistency? No, only a Horatian trick.

You say, 'I don't go in for adultery.' No, and neither do I for stealing, when I prudently pass by the silver. Take away the risk, and the bridle's off; nature leaps forth whither she will.

It is not clear whether Horace actually denies the charge or whether Davus withdraws it on his own initiative. Either way it seems that in his eagerness to prove his paradox he has been treating Horace as a representative master without regard for his individual characteristics.

After some generalities sex resurges in line 89:

A woman demands five talents[21] from you, ill-treats you, drives you from her door, douses you with cold water, calls you back. Snatch your neck out of the shameful yoke. Come on, say 'I'm a free man, yes, a free man.' You can't! A harsh master dominates your mind, puts in the goad when you are weary, pulls you about when you won't budge.

This time, no denial. Horace eschews adultery (and brothels —as a successful man he would have no use for the latter

---

[20] The ostensible message of the Epistle to Numicius; see pp. 62f.

[21] Say £5,000. Apart from metrical convenience, the Greek currency is reminiscent of Comedy.

anyway); for the rest, we remember the 'thousand passions for girls, thousands for boys' from Satires II.3. Here the large sum the lady asks for shows that Horace is flying high. From a man still only half way through his thirties such admissions would not shock friends or public; many would like him the better. The facts were probably common knowledge anyway. It is all very well to repudiate in horrified disgust the story in the Suetonian Life about Horace's erotic use of mirrors on the not entirely conclusive ground that much the same story is told of other people (he did not have to be the first to do it or the last). Augustus' name for him, 'purest of penises',[22] can hardly be dismissed as a merely visual conceit.

The allegation that Horace is over-fond of good eating is pursued at some length (102–11) and again not disavowed. 'So much,' says the unregenerate reader 'for that puritanical old farmer. Ofellus or no Ofellus, the little man is no Malvolio.' I suppose that is what Horace meant him to say. As for the truth:

That the poet is not describing himself with any consistency is clear from ll. 102ff., where he is accused of gluttony, whereas we know that he was very abstemious (cf. *Sat.* 1.5.7–9).[23]

Do we now? The lines in evidence tell us merely that at an inn on the way to Brundisium Horace went without any supper because the water was abominable. We also know that he was fat,[24] and his love of good living further appears from Epistles 1.7.35, if I interpret there correctly,[25] and Epistles 1.15. So what of the praises of simple fare? Brought to book, Horace had an easy way out: 'So it's as Davus says, I am not a pattern of consistency.'[26] But he has left a loophole. Perhaps, as with the adultery charge, Davus was not

[22] *Purissimus penis (Vita Horatii)*.

[23] H. R. Fairclough in his introductory note (Loeb Classics) to this satire. Courbaud (p. 37) quotes the same passage as evidence of Horace's delicate health: 'Un soir même, il se met à la diète.' But it was Virgil, not Horace, whose digestion gave trouble (line 49).

[24] *Epist.* 1.4.15 and the *Vita*.

[25] See pp. 54f.

[26] 'Virtually everything Horace treated presented itself to him in a double aspect' (Commager, p. 104). The section of Commager's book headed 'Balance of attitude' is particularly worth reading.

talking to Horace *sub specie Horatii*. That is what respectably-minded commentators from Porphyrio on like to maintain. Horace allows this option, but can hardly be said to encourage it. Earlier (22–4) he virtually admits that though he lauds the standards of old Rome he does not live by them. And the satire's conclusion, following directly upon the gluttony charge, is unambiguously *ad hominem*[27] (111–18):

'Add that you can't endure your own company for an hour, can't lay out your free time properly, that you shun yourself like a vagabond runaway, seeking to cheat care now with wine, now with sleep, to no purpose. The black companion treads at your heels, dogs your flight.'

'I want a stone.'

'What for?'

'Arrows!'

'The man's gone crazy, or else he's making verses.'

'Unless you take yourself off this minute, you'll be number nine on the Farm.'

'How sure of himself he must have been to amuse himself by presenting readers with such a travesty of his personality!' So Kiessling—Heinze.

---

[27] There could be a traditional element in all this. 'To judge from the very imperfect transmission the poems of Lucilius contained in abundance the sensualist's rollicking description of pleasures and passions and also the moralising satirist's condemnation of those of others . . . No one in antiquity, so far as we know, accused him of inconsistency, let alone hypocrisy' (M. Coffey, *Roman Satire* (1976), p. 52). But this is treacherous ground.

CHAPTER FOUR

The Wolf, the Tree, the Lightning, and the God

THE three Books of Horace's Odes (a fourth was to come many years later) appeared in 23. In one sense they are a continuation of the Epodes. Having naturalised the metres and spirit of Archilochian iambics, he turned to the masters of early Greek lyric, especially Alcaeus, Anacreon, and, less obviously, Pindar; three poets each with a sharply defined individuality quite unlike the other two. Hence, at least in part, the protean character of the collection. Most of the Odes are person to person, with named addressees. Sometimes these are gods or goddesses—nine of the eighty-eight are hymns. As a rule the mortal names do not count for a great deal. Visible behind his guises, as lover or spectator of love, reveller, friend, philosophic mentor, propagandist, patriot, courtier, bard, is the ever-controlling and supremely self-controlled artist. Behind the artist was a personality barely now to be glimpsed, eternally elusive.

So what of the time-worn question: Where is the real Horace? In the Anacreontic love-poems, making up about twenty-five per cent of the total, the banquet scenes and invitations, the reminders of transience and death (a new motif)? Or in praises, carried over from the Satires, of simplicity, contentment, self-sufficiency and the Golden Mean, with correlated denunciations of avarice and luxury? Or in the eulogies of those virtuous, valorous old Roman times in which Horace would not have wanted to live and of their would-be restorer, Caesar Augustus? It can be argued that these facets are not directly opposed to one another.

May not a poet sing of wine and women (also boys) within permissible limits (Horace's literary entanglements never brought him within the pale of the lex Iulia de adulteriis, even retrospectively)[1] and still reappear as a champion of sound morals and a lover of Emperor and Fatherland? The lyre attunes itself to different moods and seasons. But no, the gap is too wide for comfort, the question persists, the answer must be subjective. Here let it be that Horace invests in his standard themes as a limited partner. If the metaphor may be varied, his eggs are honest eggs, but he does not put too many in one basket and some of them stay shut away in the refrigerator. The real Horace of the Odes is the artist. When his gift, fulfilled in the taking of infinite pains, transmutes commonplace, the Odes are great poetry; when that does not happen, they can be enjoyed like the finest in eighteenth-century furniture. The gift, the Muse, is *their* reality. Having once disclaimed the name of poet, Horace has become *vates*.

Moving on this higher plane, he is no longer concerned with self-portrayal. The Horatian ethos, the irony, humour, sense—these are still here, but without any flavour of contrivance. He had long ago outlived the nervous need to make a favourable personal impression. Only a very few of the Odes turn upon a particular personal experience, and in these the experience is so presented as to warn us against taking it too seriously.

The two opening stanzas of the famous *Integer vitae* (1.22) have every appearance of solemnity:[2] the man of upright life and clean hands needs no weapons for his protection, however distant and dangerous the regions through which he travels. This absurdity,[3] as Nisbet—Hubbard austerely term the idea, is supported with an illustration: wandering unarmed in the Sabine hills and singing of his Lalage,

[1] Not to count the early Epode 8.

[2] Nisbet—Hubbard tell us that 'the Ode was even supplied with mournful music by F. F. Flemming (cf. the *Scottish students' song-book*), and sung at German and Scandinavian funerals'. According to Fraenkel (p. 184), the first stanza (only) was sung in many German schools 'at the funeral services in Hall' (presumably a regular feature of German school-life in those days).

[3] *Dulce est desipere in loco.* One thinks of Faunus' festival, when the wolf ambles about among the fearless lambs (*Odes* III.18.13; cf. 1.17.1–12).

Horace had met a wolf, which ran away. Credible enough;
but this was no ordinary wolf. The description of the animal
occupies a stanza. It is unmistakably parodic:

A monster like nothing fostered in the broad oakwoods of soldierly
Apulia nor engendered by Juba's land, arid nurse of lions.

The two final stanzas balance the two initial ones: Whether
Horace finds himself at the North Pole or the Equator, he
will always love sweet-laughing, sweet-talking Lalage.

As has been recognised, the latter part of the poem alludes
to a motif familiar in love-elegy, that lovers lead charmed
lives (as poets are said to do in Odes III.4.29–36). Granted
that Horace does not mean to be taken very seriously, the
transition from *integer vitae* to Lalage's lover leaves a hiatus[4]
—unless a link can be supplied. Perhaps it is to be found in
an almost equally well-known poem by Catullus, with whose
work Horace was certainly well acquainted, however much
or little he admired it. Catullus 76, which may be called the
first Latin love-elegy, starts with the claim that the poet's
past is free from reproach and ends with a prayer that if he
has lived a clean life the gods may liberate him from his
baneful passion for Lesbia.

Si vitam puriter egi: *integer vitae scelerisque purus*.[5] By 'living
cleanly' and by his repeated claim to be *pius* Catullus means
that he has been a faithful and honourable lover. He makes
that perfectly clear. With any other aspect of conduct he is
simply not concerned. Horace's assumption of exactly the
same attitude, when he equates an upright life and clean
hands in the first line of his ode with undying love for Lalage
in the last two ('Ring-Composition'), is a gentle mockery, not

---

[4] Not, I think, bridged by Nisbet—Hubbard's comment: 'To achieve symmetry
with the opening stanza we expect Horace to say that he will keep his heart pure;
this is what is required by the principles of "Ring-Composition" . . . Instead he
makes the less pretentious statement: "I shall go on loving Lalage." The *integer
vitae* is thus revealed as the lover; the poem which began so pompously is shown to
be not so earnest after all.'

[5] This connexion had already been suggested, along with other Catullan remi-
niscences in this ode, by M. O. Lee (*Ramus* 4 (1975), 40f.), who interprets it rather
differently.

of himself but of monopolistic love-poetry.[6] In that light the poem becomes an integrated structure, and, as Nisbet—Hubbard say, one of Horace's most charming and most perfect.

*

Like the wolf that ran away, the tree which nearly killed the poet on his Sabine farm is introduced with a parody of grand style (II.13):

Whosoever planted you, Tree, on a day of evil omen and fostered you with sacrilegious hand for the ruin of posterity and the shame of the village, well I wot that he broke his sire's neck and splashed an inner chamber with the blood of a night-slain guest. He handled poisons of Colchis and every wickedness conceived by man, he that put you, sinister timber, on my land to fall upon your innocent master.

Horace refers to this happening more than once elsewhere, so he is not very likely to have invented it. In this ode it only leads him to the thought of the great lyric poets, Sappho and Alcaeus, whom he would have met in the Underworld, and hence of the magical power of poetry. In III.4.27 the same incident is brought up along with two earlier close shaves to prove that the poet is under the protection of the Muses. We are under no compulsion to believe that he seriously believed any such thing.[7]

*

His 'conversion' in 1.34 has likewise sometimes been received with an owlish credulity which would hugely have diverted him. In the past, says this ode, the poet has been lax in religious observance, an adept of 'crazy wisdom' (meaning the materialistic doctrine of Epicurus), but now he has boxed the compass, returning to the old pieties:

---

[6] On Horace's rejection of the conventions of love-elegy see Nisbet—Hubbard II, p. 136.

[7] Heinze's portentous rhetoric is quoted and deflated by Fraenkel (p. 167 n.1).

For Light-Father [Jupiter], who generally splits *clouds* with his
flashing fire, through blue sky he drove his thundering steeds and
flying chariot, that shakes brute earth, wandering rivers, Styx,
hated Taenarus' grim crag, Atlas' boundary.

Again the bombastic language invites a sceptical response,
though if Horace had really seen what he claims it might
pass as no more than adequate. Aristotle[8] knew that lightning[9] does not occur in a clear sky, as did also scientifically
serious Latin writers (Lucretius, Seneca). But poets patron-
ised a convention that this could happen as an omen, like
other paranormal phenomena. For example, Virgil in his
Georgics[10] records it (in quantities never previously sur-
passed) among the portents which followed the assassination
of Julius Caesar. Any Jew Apella who might choose to take
Horace's story at face value was at liberty to do so. Others
would comprehend that the lightning, like the conversion,
has a purely poetic status, ad hoc.

*

The same is yet more obviously true of the hymn to Bacchus
(II.19) which begins:

I saw Bacchus (believe, posterity!) teaching songs among sequestered rocks, and nymphs at school, and the prick ears of goat-footed
satyrs.

'I think Horace means what he says. He did see Dionysus . . .
He had only to close his eyes to see the god before him, not
as a dim figure, but life-like in his beauty and strength, and
with him nymphs, satyrs . . .' I think Fraenkel[11] means what
he says.

---

[8] *Meteor.* II.9, 369b.
[9] Lightning (or a thunderbolt) is clearly implied, though scholars like to talk
merely of thunder, e.g. (out of many) A. D. Nock, *Conversion* (1933), p. 11: 'Horace
tells how he . . . was converted by a thunderclap out of a clear sky.'
[10] 1.487f.   [11] P. 200.

CHAPTER FIVE

The Letters (Book I)

By inference from the nineteenth Epistle, addressed for an obvious reason[1] to Maecenas, 'the only thoroughly bitter document that we have from Horace's pen',[2] it has often been held that Horace was deeply disappointed by the reception of his Odes.[3] The letter, if capable of that construction, is far from demanding it. The opening is light-hearted: Water-drinkers cannot make poetry; poets must drink wine.

'To sobersides I shall deny the right to sing.' From the moment I put out this edict, poets have never stopped competitive night-time soaking and daytime reeking.

And so to a tirade against imitators:

Oh you imitators, slavish herd! How often your antics have made me rage, how often they have made me laugh!

Thence by way of contrast to an affirmation of his own originality in the Epodes and Odes. Only after thirty-four lines do we arrive at the topic of public relations, which occupies the last fifteen.

Would you like to know why ungrateful readers praise and affect my little works at home, but run them down unfairly once across the threshold?

---

[1] As Horace's principal literary *fautor*. Not to show that 'he trusts him absolutely' or to show his confidence that 'Maecenas understands the value of the new poems, whatever the majority of the Roman public may think of them' (Fraenkel, p. 310).   [2] Fraenkel, p. 350.

[3] 'He vents his anger at the reception with which his odes have met' (Fraenkel, p. 310). See, however, Perret, pp. 130f., Becker, pp. 43–5 (who, however, speaks later (p. 49 n. 9) of 'der geringe Publikumserfolg der Oden'), Williams, pp. 24–8, R. Kilpatrick, *Phoenix* 29 (1975), 117–27.

The answer given is that Horace has declined to buy popularity with dinner-parties and little presents or by mixing with the 'literary set'. *Hinc illae lacrimae.* The letter ends with a characteristic manoeuvre:

If I say that I am too modest to recite my unworthy compositions to crowded halls and attach weight to trifles, says he: 'You jest. You keep them for Jove's[4] ears, for you're sure that you are the only one who distils poetic honey. How you fancy yourself!' I dare not sneer in reply—don't want a scratching from my antagonist's sharp fingernails. 'I don't like this venue', I say and demand an intermission. For sport has been known to breed eager strife and anger, and from anger come savage feuds and calamitous war.

The antagonist is, of course, perfectly correct. Horace does *not* think of his work as 'trifles', unworthy of wide publicity. That had been made sufficiently clear in Satire 1.10, as in lines 76f.

Not I. 'The Knights applaud me, that's all I want', as saucy Arbuscula[5] said when she was hissed off the stage, despising the rest.

Here, however, he lets the imaginary carper make the point, and by way of an added refinement has himself accused of arrogance, not without an allusion to the Emperor's patronage. His own smiling evasion of the charge[6] amounts to a shrug. Like Housman, he would rather be arrogant than impudent.

The interpretation of Letter 19 as an ebullition of chagrin at the public's failure to appreciate the Odes properly must be restrained by a number of considerations. (1) The Odes are mentioned, along with the Epodes, only in vindication of Horace's claim to originality. (2) If he had the Odes primarily in mind, the tirade against imitators implies that the publication had set a new literary fashion[7]—not a sign of

---

[4] The Emperor's.

[5] An actress seen on stage by Cicero in 54.

[6] 'It is without a smile that we are dismissed at the end of this letter' (Fraenkel (p. 350), who failed to realise that the prim sententiousness of the last two lines is tongue-in-cheek).

[7] Fraenkel (p. 341 n. 1) points to the Pindarising Titius of *Epist.* 1.3.9. Jullus Antonius, addressed in *Odes* IV.2, seems to have followed in the same wake.

neglect. (3) Horace deals with critics and detractors as he dealt with them in Satire 1.10, with less of explicit contempt but with the added imputation of dishonesty—privately, he says, they admire his work. If, again, the Odes are in mind, what else had he expected of Tigellius Hermogenes and the literary rabble?[8] There is no hint in the letter that the persons whose judgment Horace had professed in the Satire (81–90) to value, to say nothing of the 'imitators', had been less than enthusiastic about the Odes—unless silence is a hint. For, after all, the theory may not be entirely wrong. Perhaps Horace *had* imagined that the Odes would make an even greater immediate impact than in fact they did, silencing the carpers at last. That was not to be,[9] not at least until after Caesar Augustus, whose continued approval is quietly intimated in line 43, had chosen Horace to compose the hymn for his Secular Festival—and not altogether even then.

*

Be that as it may, nothing could be less plausible than to make disgruntlement the reason why Horace for the time being turned away from lyric poetry. Three Books of it were enough for him and his public. The grand epilogue (Odes III.30) beginning 'I have completed a monument more enduring than bronze' implies that he looked upon his work in that area as done. But writing verse was his métier: 'Whatever my life's style, I shall go on writing.'[10] Moreover, it was expected of him. Perhaps his next venture, the series of twenty letters in hexameter verse known as the first Book of Epistles, had its origin in letters actually so composed and sent for the amusement of himself and his correspondents, like those which Spurius Mummius sent home from Corinth in 146 and which remained in the possession of his family in Cicero's time.[11] But the verse-letter seems also to have been

---

[8] *Ventosa plebes* of line 37. Not, I think, the man in the street. Dinner invitations and presents would be for people more or less active in literary circles.

[9] Cf. *Epist.* I.14.37f.: 'Nobody there in the country scrapes away at my blessings squint-eyed or pursues them with the bite of hidden hate.'

[10] *Sat.* II.1.60.

[11] *Ad Att.* XIII.6.4.

an established literary form,[12] and nearly all of Horace's
were clearly written as literature, whether or not they were
ever despatched to the addressees. Several are moral discourses, practically indistinguishable from satires of that
type (Horace uses the same term *sermones* for both), except
for the absence of unflattering personal references.[13] Most
are didactic in one way or another. Courbaud may have been
right to see in the Epistles a distinctively Horatian combination, stemming from the prose epistolary treatise, like those
of Epicurus, on one side and a non-didactic verse-letter
tradition on the other.[14]

The first Letter, addressed once again to Maecenas, prepares the ground. It purports to be a farewell to poetry.[15]
Horace professes to have no philosophical commitments—he
leans now towards the Stoics now towards their adversaries
—but claims an ardent desire to immerse himself in philosophical study. The lecture that follows retreads well-worn
tracks—the folly of greed and ambition, the inconsistency of
mankind in general. He has nothing really new to offer on
these subjects, but handles them with all his old picturesque
versatility and a new smoothness and ease, an apparently
effortless command of phrase and metre,[16] a comfortable
good humour like a cat purring on the hearthrug, the full
maturity of his technique.

Three letters are addressed to Maecenas, the first, seventh
and nineteenth. Both the first two present the poet as de-
clining to fall in with a wish of his patron's. In the first Letter
he tells Maecenas that he will write no more poetry because
'my age is not what it was, neither is my mind.' In the
seventh Maecenas' desire to have him in Rome is refused on
the same grounds: 'If you want me never to leave you, you

---

[12] Lucil. (Marx) 181, 341. Cf. Catull. 38, 68.

[13] Gargilius and Mutus in *Epist.* 6 are throwbacks.

[14] P. 29: 'En prenant ses modèles à droite et à gauche, chez les auteurs de simples
billets en vers comme chez les savants redacteurs d'*Epistolicae quaestiones*, Horace a
créé quelque chose qui ne ressemble à rien de ce qui existait avant lui.'

[15] *Versus* in line 10 precludes application to lyric poetry only. It is sometimes
overlooked that *Epist.* 1 may be the last or among the last in order of composition.

[16] Never better described than by Horace himself, *A. p.* 240–2 *ex noto fictum carmen
sequar, ut sibi quivis/speret idem, sudet multum frustraque laboret/ausus idem.*

must give me back my youth.' Highly interesting in its personal aspects, this seventh Letter is the most controversial of the series.

It opens with a plain statement: 'I promised you that I should take five days in the country, but I lied; you have missed me all through August.' His excuse: he is afraid to risk his health in Rome at this time of year. But as Fraenkel says, the parodic exaggeration with which he makes this plea, shows that it is not too seriously meant. Then (10–13):

> When winter spreads snow over the Alban fields, your poet will go down to the sea-side and cosset himself and read huddled up in retirement. You, dear friend, he will revisit with the west winds, if you permit, and the first swallow.

'If you permit': that is, 'if you are willing to see me.' Maecenas' leave for the half-year absence is *not* sought, though he could take it that way at first if he chose. But the following twenty-six lines are a declaration of independence:

> You did not make me rich after the manner of the Calabrian who encouraged his guest to eat his pears. 'Eat them, do.' 'I've had enough'. 'Well, but take away all you like.' 'No really, thanks'. 'It will make a nice present for the youngsters.' 'I am as much obliged as if I went off loaded with them.' 'As you like. If you leave them, they'll only go straight to the pigs.' He who gives away what he dislikes and despises is a prodigal and a fool. That field yields nothing but ingratitude, and ever will. The good and wise man says he is ready for the worthy,[17] but he knows the difference between real money and make-belief. I too shall prove myself worthy, for the credit of my deserving patron.

Fraenkel's elaborate discussion[18] is convincing in the main, but less so on 22f.:

> *vir bonus et sapiens dignis ait esse paratus,*
> *nec tamen ignorat quid distent aera lupinis.*

A *vir bonus et sapiens*, and so Maecenas, puts his benefactions at the disposal of persons who are worthy of them and at the same time he knows very well the difference between real coins and sham coins,

---

[17] I.e. ready to give generously.
[18] Pp. 329–32.

between true benefactions and gifts that merely look like benefactions. Such a man will endow only those of whose gratitude he can be sure, but—this is clearly implied by the whole context—he will not exploit the gratitude of his friends so as to present them with gifts of doubtful value.

I think Horace's meaning can be made plainer in fewer words. *Vir bonus et sapiens*, and so Maecenas, is ready to give to the deserving, and yet he knows the value of his gifts (and so does not scatter them broadcast). Thus *tamen*, which exercised Fraenkel and others, has full adversative force. In line 24,

dignum praestabo me etiam pro laude merentis,

etiam is not easy to fix. I take it as = *quoque* ('I, like your other protégés'), but it could relate to what goes before ('I too on my side') or be understood with Orelli as *etiam propterea ut collaudetur ab aliis is quem dignis favere vident*. He seems to take *pro* as in *pro patria mori*, which best suits the context, despite Lucretius 5.1f. *dignum . . . carmen/pro rerum maiestate* et sim. As Fraenkel says, Epistles II.1.246f. can be helpfully compared: *munera quae multa dantis cum laude tulerunt/dilecti tibi Vergilius Variusque poetae*. At all events, Horace undertakes to do his patron credit.

Details aside, this passage is to say that Maecenas and Horace represent a model patron-protégé relationship. Now the rub: 'But if I am to be with you all the time, you must make me young again' (the theme of youth is elaborated over three lines). Horace cannot and will not be at Maecenas' beck and call. Rather than that, *cuncta resigno*: he will return everything Maecenas has given him (29–34). This is conveyed by the fable of the fox[19] who gorged herself in a corn-bin with the result that she could not get out through the hole that let her in.

I don't praise the common man's slumbers[20] when I am full of fatted fowl, neither am I willing to exchange the full freedom of my leisure for all the wealth of Araby (35f.).

---

[19] Or dormouse (*nitedula*), if Bentley is followed.
[20] Plain eater makes sound sleeper; cf. *Sat.* II.2.80f.

Line 35 is generally understood as a declaration of sincerity ('let no one think that when he says *cuncta resigno* he is carried away by a theoretical enthusiasm for poverty or is making a false pretence like those *qui Curios simulant et Bacchanalia vivunt*').[21] I suggest that it is better taken as an instance of 'the fairly common form of *comparatio paratactica*, where, according to our way of thinking, we should subordinate the first parallel clause to the second'.[22] That is to say, while Horace admits that he enjoys the good things money buys, does not pretend to like poverty for its own sake, he will not give up his independence for any amount of money.

You have often praised my backwardness in asking favours and I have called you 'patron' and 'father' to your face, nor said a word less behind your back. Look and see if I can cheerfully restore what you have bestowed (37–9).

Horace has never been greedy or demanding. That goes to show that he can do without if need arise. But how is his gratitude to Maecenas relevant at this point? I suppose it simply reinforces *verecundum* ('my backwardness in asking favours'). He might have asked for more, but has been thankful for what he got—never a grumble. So Maecenas can be sure that he can resign it all without repining.

Now the letter takes a new tack and the rest of it is calculated to soften the abrasiveness of 29–39—of that more presently. But those eleven lines are critical. More than any other part of Horace's work the Epistles divide convictions on the reality and importance of factual background, with the range running from Fraenkelian fundamentalism[23] to radical negation.[24] Letter 7 is exceptional in that the situation it presents has the aspect of a major personal crisis, with

[21] Fraenkel, p. 334.   [22] Ibid. p. 398.

[23] Perhaps to some extent inherited from Courbaud.

[24] In Becker's view (p. 46): 'Even of the letters which appear to arise out of a clearly defined "real" situation or to have a specific purpose, none attempts to reach into the recipient's life or impel him into concrete action.' And on Letter 7 (p. 37): 'Maecenas could not see in the letter a menacing, momentous communication, which he was expected to answer and "guarantee Horace his freedom". He received it as a work of literature, a poem.' Similarly McGann (pp. 95f.): 'It is a discussion, cast in epistolary form, of the issues which can arise when an aging dependant is drawn away from the side of his great friend and seeks the peace of the

Horace telling his benefactor after some fifteen years of close friendship that he is ready to give up all past bounties rather than compromise his freedom, which is *ex hypothesi* in danger. Here at least the question 'reality or fiction?' refuses to be shelved as immaterial to literary appreciation.

It stands to reason that the letter as we have it was not despatched only a few weeks after Horace left Rome. An acknowledged masterpiece, it will have been the product of much filing. But he might have sent an essentially similar letter to Maecenas at the time, even put it into verse as a way of softening the impact. However, the letter is not to be considered as the private communication which it could originally have been, but as a manifesto. At the beginning of the first Epistle Horace intimates that he is his own man, able to decline a request from Maecenas, but he does it inoffensively. In the seventh independence is almost aggressively asserted. In the Satires he was out to draw attention to the relationship while at the same time (at least in the first Book) blunting the teeth of Envy. Now he is telling Rome that it does not make him a lackey. There are kind words for Maecenas, but the message is not compromised to spare his feelings, which we are at liberty to imagine. Of course, he must have consented to the publication. 'Not perhaps in the best of taste,' Maecenas may have thought, 'after all I have done for him. Would he have written it I wonder, in my palmier days?[25] But it would be petty to object. It's certainly one of the best things he has done.' For surely the crisis *was* imaginary, or at any rate exaggerated out of all proportion to reality. Otherwise Maecenas must have been really hurt and Horace's behaviour becomes inexcusable, except in the

---

countryside . . . There is no justification for believing that Horace has revealed a difficult situation existing between Maecenas and himself. *Cuncta resigno* has no more connection with a real world of plans and intentions than has another declaration addressed to Maecenas, *Odes* III.16.22ff.' Maybe so. But was this evident to the ordinary reader? Did Horace mean it to be evident?

[25] Maecenas seems to have lost ground with the Emperor following the execution of his brother-in-law Varro Murena in 22. After the publication of the first Book of Epistles his name disappears from Horace's writings except for one affectionate reference in the fourth Book of Odes. Maecenas' message to Augustus in his will, 'Remember Horatius Flaccus as you remember me', may not have been entirely innocent of *sous-entendu*.

eyes of the faithful for whom he can do no wrong. Some of these choose to suppose that Maecenas had provoked him by a tactless reminder of his obligations, but that is not implied in the letter. Even if it were so, anything Maecenas may have written remained between him and Horace. Moreover, *he* had a legitimate complaint in that Horace by his own admission had broken a promise.

On a literal interpretation the offer to 'give it all back' is insulting. As though Maecenas would have wanted that! Also dishonest, because impracticable. Over and beyond material benefits, Horace was indebted to his patron for things which perhaps meant even more to him, status, a place in high society ('association with the great'), things which could not be returned. Certainly Horace had done his part *pro laude merentis* but that was not the issue. Moreover, by this time Horace no longer depended on Maecenas. Besides the Sabinum, he had acquired a place at Tibur, perhaps another at Tarentum. These may even have become his favourites.[26] From Letter 14 he appears to have had an establishment in Rome as well with staff permanently attached. And he stood well with the Emperor, no less, who was generous from time to time.[27] Let him then be acquitted of having exploited a truly painful personal situation. He imagined it, or most of it, the more readily perhaps because indifference to fortune's comings and goings had become one of his staple themes,[28] to make a delightful piece of writing (so long as personal implications are not too closely scrutinised) and to give the world notice that Quintus Horatius Flaccus was at his own disposal. That may not be all, however. But first, the rest of the letter.

At line 40 we move on to ground already prepared in 25–8. Rome with its festivities and social chores, its petitioners and celebrities and multitudinous contacts, is no longer for Horace. What Maecenas offers him there is like the horses offered to Ulysses' son in the *Odyssey*, a magnificent present but inappropriate. 'Little things suit little men. It is not

[26] See H. Hommel, *Horaz* (1950), pp. 124f.
[27] *Vita Horatii.*
[28] Cf. *Epist.* 1.1.68f., 6.5ff., 10.30ff., 16.73ff.

queenly Rome that pleases me nowadays but empty Tibur
and peace-loving Tarentum' (he could scarcely include the
Sabinum, which was part of the proffered refund). Without
further preamble the letter ends with the longest of Horatian
anecdotes, told with a wealth of vivid detail. In brief: As
Philippus, described as a hard-working and famous barrister,
certainly a person of wealth and social distinction,[29] is on his
way home from the Forum, he happens to notice a man
cleaning his nails in the shade of a barber's shop and takes it
into his head to invite him to dinner. He turns out to be an
auctioneer[30] by the name of Vulteius Mena. Mena finally
accepts the invitation and becomes a regular dinner-guest
and client. One day his patron takes him on a trip into the
Sabine countryside. Never having been out of the big city
before (we gather), Mena is enchanted. Much amused,
Philippus persuades him to turn farmer. Set up on a farm at
his patron's expense, Mena takes to his new career with
enthusiasm;[31] but everything goes wrong, crops and livestock perish. Angry and disheartened, he rides off to Rome
in the middle of the night and implores Philippus to let him
go back to his old way of life. The moral follows, or rather
two interrelated morals:

Let him who has once seen how much superior are the things he
let go to the things he pursued return while there is still time and
seek again what he left behind. It is best for each one of us to
measure himself by his own rod and rule.

---

[29] If L. Marcius Philippus, Consul in 91, is intended (which, however, seems to
me very doubtful), he was a great noble and one of the leading politicians of the
period. It might as well be borne in mind that he had a son, Consul in 56 and
Augustus' stepfather; and there were other contemporary members of the family.
But I suspect that Horace invented the name and the story.

[30] *Praeco.* As such he stood low in the Roman social scale.

[31] 83–5. Line 85, *immoritur studiis et amore senescit habendi*, is always misunderstood.
Habendi does not=*lucri* ('getting rich'), as in Ov. *Met.* 1.131 *amor sceleratus habendi.*
Nothing suggests that Mena is a money-grubber; he is obsessed with the pride and
joy of owning land. For this sense of *habere* cf. Cic. *Ad fam.* XVI.21.7 *habes* ('you are
a landed proprietor'), also *Harvard stud. cl. phil.* 83 (1979), 247 on another mis-
handled passage, Cic. *Verr.* II.3.95 *omnis qui haberent in Sicilia.* *Senescit*, like *immoritur*,
connotes protracted absorption; cf. *Epist.* II.2.82f. *et studiis annos septem dedit in-
senuitque/libris et curis.*

As an illustration of the second maxim the anecdote is fully appropriate. The first takes us back to Horace's *cuncta resigno*; improperly, because there could be no question of Horace going back to the life he led before Maecenas took him in hand. None the less, the story with its patron-client framework cannot but evoke Horace and Maecenas. Fraenkel treats it as a straightforward paradigm. Philippus 'appears as the distinguished public figure that he was and as a real gentleman . . . The words (79) *et sibi dum requiem, dum risus undique quaerit* ['in his search for relaxation and laughs anywhere he could find them'] must not be thought to suggest that he is merely exploiting Mena for his own amusement.'[32] Which are we to believe, Fraenkel or Horace? Philippus is a prototype of the Caliph in Flecker's *Hassan*, less sinister, of course, and in miniature; whereas Mena is a man in a Roman street, a Babbitt with neither talent nor personality to make him interesting. As parabolic counterparts of Maecenas and Horace, this sorry couple are caricatures. Perhaps it is part of their function to suggest what the Maecenas-Horace relationship was *not*.[33] Mainly, no doubt, they are there to entertain us, which they surely do, and to take some of the sting out of the early part of the letter.

It can hardly be by coincidence that two other letters in the series, placed side by side (17 and 18), deal with the theme of 'association with the great'. Both tender advice to young men otherwise unknown (except that the second, Lollius, is also the addressee of Letter 2). Horace makes no direct reference to his own experience, but his readers know that he writes *en connaissance de cause*, and in the Lollius letter there may be one or two discreet reminders. Lollius must not appear to be in competition with his patron (28 *contendere noli*, 30f. *desine mecum/certare*), the very mistake attributed to Horace in Satires II.3.307–20. He is warned not to sit writing poetry when his patron wants to go hunting (40). 'Cultivating a powerful friend sounds attractive to those who have not tried it. Experience teaches fear' (86f.). On the whole, however, the advice is general, and decidedly down to earth.

---

[32] P. 337.
[33] Cf. p. 20 on *Sat.* 1.9.

Both letters seem to imply that Horace himself is done with all that. The letter to Lollius ends significantly:

(As for me in my Sabine retreat), how do you think I feel, my friend, what do you suppose I pray for? Let me keep what is now mine, or even less. And let me live the time that remains, if the gods will that any time remain, unto myself. Let me have good store of books and fruits of the earth laid up for a coming season, and let me not sway in suspense, expectant of the uncertain hour. But it is enough to pray Jove for what Jove gives and takes away. Let him grant life and substance; peace of mind I shall provide for myself.

The half-cynical, half-mocking tone of Letter 17, to Scaeva, makes simplistic Horatians uncomfortable. First, there is that disconcerting comparison between the philosopher-courtier Aristippus, preacher of hedonism, and Diogenes, the uncouth and ridiculous Cynic, all to the advantage of the former. The advice, when it comes, amounts to a single item: 'Don't be whining for largesse all the time. You will net less that way.' A remarkable document.

Of course Horace could not mean us to infer that his relationship with Maecenas had been as sordid as what he envisages for Scaeva. But his rose-coloured spectacles are off. Neither letter so much as hints that a patron could become an understanding friend or that a client should do anything beyond humouring his patron's fancies and avoiding obvious *faux pas*, with the sole motive of worldly advantage and profit. It might almost be the 'bore' talking in riper years. The conclusion is hard to resist that behind the probably fictitious background of the seventh letter lay some degree of actual alienation, if not from Maecenas, from the dependence he represented.

*

Within the individual letters and within the Book as a whole, the autobiographical elements, the decisions in Horace's life, even his work as a poet are touched upon not for their own sake but for the sake of the ethical teachings.

So Carl Becker,[34] and it is undeniable that ethical teachings, though I regard them as a means to maintain the flow of Horatian verse rather than as an end, take the lion's share in the Epistles. The meagre stock of moral commonplace repeats itself in forms ingeniously varied. Occasionally the flow seems automatic, the intellectual control relaxed. Letter 14, to the bailiff of the Sabine farm (a slave, as bailiffs always or normally were), starts with a challenge (4f.):

Let us see which of the two of us plucks out thorns more vigorously, you from the land or I from the mind, and whether Horace or his acres are in better shape.

Excellent, but nothing much to do with the rest.

I have to stay in Rome to comfort a bereaved friend, but would like to be in the country. You say happiness is in town. Both discontented, both fools. It's the mind, not the place, that's wrong (6–13, summary).

A familiar thesis, the theme of another letter (11). But in the main section of this one (14–42) Horace deserts it. Summary:

However, when you were in town, you wanted a job in the country; now you want to get back. I, on the other hand, am consistent, as you know. The fact is, our tastes differ. You want the cookhouses and the girls. I, who enjoyed the social life well enough in my younger days, now hanker for peace and quiet.

So whereabouts do matter, after all, as they do in Letter 7. Incidentally, the three verses (32–4) looking back on vanished youth parallel 25–8 of that letter, even to the nostalgic evocation of long-lost Cinara. Horace's claim to consistency can be set against Satires II.7.28f. ('at Rome you pray for the country, but when in the country you turn about and laud the absent city to the skies') and Epistles I.8.12 ('in Rome I love Tibur, in Tibur, ever fickle I love Rome'). Moral progress?[35] If so, apparently not lasting. Some years later he writes in the Epistle to Florus

---

[34] P. 48 (here and occasionally elsewhere I have translated from the German).

[35] So Courband, pp. 158f.: 'Ainsi Horace voit clair en lui désormais, et ne doute plus de ses préférences, et tient à ce qu'on en soit convaincu. Établir définitivement ce point, ce sera le premier objet de sa lettre.'

(Epistles ii.2.65–76, a passage strongly reminiscent of Satires ii.6.20ff.):

Apart from all else, do you think I can write poetry in Rome amongst so many worries and labours? One man summons me to stand surety, another to listen to his compositions, all other duties left aside. Then there are the invalids, one on the Quirinal, the other at the far end of the Aventine, both to be visited—you notice the spacing, how thoughtfully convenient! Ah, but the streets are clear, nothing to get in the way of meditation. Well, the hustling contractor dashes along with his mules and porters, a crane whirls a block of stone or a huge log in the air, sorrowing funerals struggle with sturdy wagons, a mad dog flees one way, a muddy sow plunges another: make up melodious verses if you can!

The excuse would be idle if Horace were not spending most of his life in Rome, which so late in his career he would hardly be doing against his will.

Letter 14 concludes:

(You prefer city rations) but the footman envies you your use of the wood, the livestock, the kitchen garden. The lazy ox wants to wear harness, the nag covets the plough. To both my advice will be: practice what you know and be cheerful in it.

The final maxim, another echo of Letter 7 (or vice versa), settles nothing for the bailiff, who knew both town and country, or for his master either. This is a poem to be enjoyed rather than analysed.

None of the series has caused so much perplexity as the sixth, to Numicius, 'the most elaborate, the most enigmatical, and the most impersonal of all the ethical Epistles'.[36] Its first twenty-seven lines, directed against people who let outward things impress them, are unremarkable, except for one striking thought, which Horace seems to throw out casually and never develops: 'The Sage would be dubbed madman if he sought virtue itself to excess.' Then he takes an odd turn (28–32):

If acute disease attacks your lungs or kidneys, seek escape from that disease. You want to live right. Who doesn't? If virtue alone

---

[36] Sellar, p. 95.

can produce this, then be strong, give up your pet fancies and get down to business. Do you take virtue for words and a sacred wood for so much timber? Then see to it that no man make port ahead of you.

So on for another thirty-five lines: if wealth or honours or good eating or sex mean most to a man, let him pursue it for all he is worth. 'Is this all irony, or serious advice?' Neither, entirely. These mundane pursuits are implicitly condemned by the terms in which they are recommended:[37]

If to dine well is to live well, the sun is up, let us go where our gullets lead us . . . Let us bathe bloated from an undigested meal, oblivious of the decencies (56–62).

And yet there is a serious substratum to the advice. The doctrine that consistency in a bad course is preferable to instability was preached by Davus in Satires II.7.15–20. Its advocacy here is not totally ironic, nor yet a *reductio ad absurdum*. There *is* something to be said for doing thoroughly what you do. But Horace is not really interested in ethical complexities. He has found a new angle. The lively descriptions of the different avocations are just literature.

Moral counsel abounds in the Epistles, but as in the Satires Horace time and again plays down the unappealing role of mentor. Letter 8 is an admission of failure to live up to his own standards:

If he asks after me, tell him I make many fine promises but live neither rightly nor agreeably (3–4).

Letter 10 (44–6):

Live like a sage, Aristius, happy in your lot, nor leave me unrebuked when you think I am garnering more than I need and never stopping.

Two letters, 4 and 15, are unabashedly Epicurean. The close of the latter runs in line with 7.35 ('I don't praise the common man's slumbers when I'm full of fatted fowl'):[38]

---

[37] As Sellar saw.　　[38] See p. 55.

I praise things safe and humble when I am out of funds and put up with cheap fare stoutly enough. But when something better and juicier comes my way, I say that you are the only sensible, right-living folk whose money we see soundly invested in handsome country houses.

And in 15.18–21 the 'sleek porker from Epicurus' herd' (4.16) is still not too old to enjoy good wine when he visits the sea-side after the simplicities of the Sabine farm:

Wine to drive away my cares, flow rich with hope into my veins and mind, put words upon my tongue, make me young and attractive to a local girl-friend.

Following a Hellenistic literary practice, the last letter, 20, addressed to the Book, ends with a 'seal' (*sphragis*), i.e. a brief sketch of the author. Before giving his date of birth Horace's runs as follows:

You will say that, born a freedman's son in modest circumstances, I spread my wings too wide for the nest, so that you add to my merits what you take from my birth. Say that in war[39] and at home I found favour with Rome's leading men; small of stature, grey-haired before my time, sun-loving, quick to anger, but willing to be appeased.

Me primis Urbis belli placuisse domique, 'Envy will reluctantly admit that I have associated with the great',[40] 'to have found favour with leading men is not the least of achievements'.[41] For all his display of independence in Letter 7 and his awareness of the seamy side of clientship in 17 and 18, Horace remained what would now be called an inveterate snob. And why not? He had reason to be proud of the fact that Maecenas and Augustus himself, men of high culture and intelligence who had all Roman society to choose from, could not get enough of his company. Augustus wrote to him:[42]

Please don't stand on ceremony with me, behave as though we were regular cronies. That will be quite proper and in order on

---

[39] Usually taken as a reference to Brutus, but perhaps ambiguous, since *Odes* III.4.28 suggests that Horace took some part in the operations against Sex. Pompeius in the thirties.

[40] *Sat.* II.1.75–77.   [41] *Epist.* I.17.35.   [42] *Vita Horatii.*

your part, since I should have liked such friendly relations if your
health would allow.

And again:

Our friend Septimius among others will tell you how I remember
you, since I happened to mention you while he was by. Your
high-and-mightiness scorned my friendship, but I do not on that
account get on my high horse in return.

A little older, a little colder. The ease, poise, and assured
technique of Horace's Letters carries them so happily
through even the most protracted sermonising that the cool-
ing of his emotional climate escapes attention. Who were
these correspondents? Omitting Maecenas, Tiberius Nero
(the Emperor's stepson and eventual successor), the bailiff,
and the Book, we are left with twelve, of whom only one,
Aristius Fuscus, is known from the Satires. Several others had
been recipients of odes.[43] The majority are mere names.
From the contents of the letters it may be doubted whether
Horace's relations with any of them amounted to more than
friendly acquaintance. Where is Virgil, 'the half of my
soul'?[44] Where are those two other beloved fellow-travellers,
Varius and Plotius? *O qui complexus et gaudia quanta fuerunt!*[45]
Horace still wears his amiable smile, but he had perhaps
grown rather weary of his world.

One of the unknowns, Bullatius of Letter 11, was travelling
in the East. Remembering his own peregrinations, Horace
asks him what he thinks of the famous islands and cities of the
Aegean and Asia Minor, Chios, Lesbos, Samos, Sardis,
Smyrna, Colophon? Or does he like little Lebedos?

You know what Lebedos is? Just a village, more empty than Gabii
and Fidenae.[46] Yet I should have liked to live there, forgetting my

---

[43] Including Albius, generally identified with the elegist Tibullus. Doubters are
contemptuously dismissed by Fraenkel (p. 323 n. 2). I still think that Postgate
(*Selections from Tibullus*, pp. 179–84) made in some respects a powerful case.

[44] *Odes* 1.3.8.

[45] *Sat* 1.5.43.

[46] 'Ghost towns' (almost) near Rome.

friends and by them to be forgotten, looking from shore far out over the raging sea (7–10).[47]

Everyone is put in mind of the beginning of Lucretius' second Book, where the wise man is pictured watching common humanity flounder, like a man safe on shore enjoying[48] the spectacle of a storm-tossed ship.[49] But Horace's primary thought is not of security on land as opposed to peril on water but of the remoteness of the little island and total severance from all familiar ties.[50] There is a breath of romanticism in the lines, recalling some of Coventry Patmore:

> Here in this little Bay,
> Full of tumultuous life and great repose,
> Where, twice a day,
> The purposeless, glad ocean comes and goes,
> Under high cliffs, and far from the huge town,
> I sit me down.
> For want of me the world's course will not fail:
> When all its work is done, the lie shall rot;
> The truth is great, and shall prevail,
> When none cares whether it prevail or not.

Something quite startling, encountered in the mundane context of a Horatian *sermo*.

---

[47] The egregious notion of the scholiasts that these lines are put by Horace into Bullatius' mouth, 'in a manner unparalleled elsewhere in the Epistles' (small wonder!), refuses to die (see McGann, p. 61, or O. A. W. Dilke in *Horace* (ed. C. D. N. Costa (1973), p. 97). Was Horace likely to mention Lebedos unless he had been there himself? In which case, would he make Bullatius tell him what he already knew?

[48] Roman realism again.

[49] Cicero uses the same image in a letter to Atticus (II.7.4).

[50] A point well taken by Courbaud, pp. 144f.

CHAPTER SIX

Ligurinus

HORACE's return to the lyre with his Secular Hymn in 17 was followed by the publication of a fourth Book of Odes, fifteen in number. The old lyric themes recur, but the proportions have changed. The national chord sounds loud and often, in celebration of the Emperor and his martial stepsons. Poetry and *vates Horatius* take a generous share. But love, wine and mortality are not forgotten. The first of the collection is addressed to the goddess of love. Horace is fifty or thereabouts; let her spare him and betake herself to the house of that accomplished young aristocrat, Paullus Fabius Maximus. Such matters are not for Horace any more—neither woman nor boy.

But why, Ligurinus, ah why does a tear ever and anon trickle down my cheeks? Why does my fluent tongue fall in mid speech into unseemly silence? At night in dreams I catch and hold you, follow you as you dart across the green in Mars' Field or through the flowing waters, cruel one!

In a paper published in 1962[1] Professor Gordon Williams maintained that Ligurinus (also addressed as a proud beauty in Ode 10 of this Book) never existed, which may well be true. Proving it is another matter.

Homosexual love, regarded with complacency in certain social strata in early Greece and become a hardened poetic convention in Alexandria, was the object of penal legislation in Rome and conventionally regarded as disgraceful.

---

[1] 'Poetry in the moral climate of Augustan Rome' (*Journ. Rom. stud.* 52 (1962), 28–46 (see 38–41)).

So when Horace and other Latin poets of his or earlier gen-
erations 'pose as *so*[*m*]*domites*' (as the Marquess of Queens-
berry put it), they are merely following a literary convention.

Granted that homosexuality probably was one of the arts
which Greece, or Magna Graecia, brought to rustic Latium,
the literary evidence to which Professor Williams invites us
to look goes nothing like so far as he suggests. First, however,
the penal legislation. A law of uncertain date, the lex
Scantinia,[2] against violation of freeborn males by males was
in existence at this period.[3] Its provisions are not known in
detail[4] and the paucity of references in our sources suggests
that it rarely came into operation.

Professor Williams appeals unto Cicero as 'typical of right-
thinking people'. To Cicero let us go. Actually, his writings
contain little of importance on this subject. Nothing can be
deduced from a reference in his defence of Milo[5] (in 52) to
the killing of an officer by a soldier whom he was attempting
to seduce—naturally a case of justifiable homicide. Scarcely
more relevant are Cicero's fulminations against Clodius,
Gabinius and Mark Antony as persons who in their youth
had prostituted themselves for gain.[6] Of Catiline he says[7]
that he loved some of the young men around him 'most
disgracefully' (*turpissime*), but the vague adverb may point
to the promiscuity of the relationships and the manner in
which Catiline exploited them rather than to their homosexual character *per se*. It is noteworthy that Cicero's tract
On friendship, concerned as it is only with friendship between
man and man, contains not a word about homosexuality.
Apparently he was simply not interested. Professor Williams
quotes (in the Latin) a passage from his *Tusculan disputations*.[8]

---

[2] For the sources see Mommsen, *Römisches Strafrecht*, 703f.

[3] Cic. *Ad fam.* VIII.14.4.

[4] Quintilian is no doubt referring to this law in *Inst.* IV.2.69. The verb he uses, *stuprare*, applies only to an active partner, whether or not acting with the consent of the passive.

[5] *Mil.* 9.

[6] Clodius: *Sest.* 39 (cf. *Ad Att.* IV.11.2). Gabinius: *Dom.* 126, *Sest.* 18, 26. Antony: *Phil.* II.44 *et al.* Cicero has a similar innuendo against young Curio in a letter to Atticus (I.14.5). A joke recorded in *De orat.* II.265 implies the like against Sex. Titius.

[7] *Catil.* II.8.   [8] IV.70f.

But let us allow the poets to amuse themselves, in whose stories we observe that Jupiter himself is mixed up in this infamy.[9] Let us go to our instructors in virtue, the philosophers, who deny that love has to do with the sexual act[10] and take issue on this point with Epicurus—who in my opinion is not far out.[11] For what is this 'love that is friendship?' Why does nobody love an ugly young man or a handsome old one? For my part, I think this practice arose in the Greek gymnasia,[12] in which such love-relationships are un-inhibited and sanctioned (so Ennius was right: 'Scandal started with the baring of their bodies, man and maid'). Even though such relationships may be chaste, as I believe is possible, they are none the less anxious and tense, the more so as the restraint and limitation are self-imposed. Again, to say nothing of the loving of women, to which nature has accorded greater license, who does not take the poet's meaning in connexion with the seizure of Ganymede or understand what Laius in Euripides says and wants? Finally, look at what fine poets, men of the highest culture, publish about themselves in their poems and songs. Alcaeus was a brave man, well-known in his community. What things he writes about the love of young men! Anacreon's entire work is erotic, while Ibycus of Rhegium was the most ardent lover of them all, as his writings make plain.

To regard the above as Cicero's judgment on homo-sexuality is mainly to misapprehend. The passage is part of a disquisition on passionate love, both heterosexual and homosexual, as one of the disorders which trouble the human psyche and of which the wise man must rid himself. Cicero combats the Stoic position that such love can in practice exist on a non-physical plane. The Stoics, being Greeks, had taken male homosexual love as typical, and Cicero follows suit. But he is also thinking of heterosexual love, as he implies by his reference to Anacreon, whose poems (like Horace's) deal in both.

When Cicero says that nature has accorded greater licence to the love of women, he leaves us guessing at precisely what he means. In his wholesale condemnation of love in the

---

[9] Erotic passion, not necessarily homosexual, and its consequences.
[10] *Stuprum*, the act as committed by one person on another.
[11] Epicurus defined love as sexual appetite.
[12] Similarly criticised in *Rep.* IV.4.

ordinary sense of the word[13] he conveniently ignores the
institution of marriage, but it may have been in the back of
his mind at this point. Furthermore, according to ordinary
Roman morality, there was nothing very wrong about a
young man having affairs with courtesans,[14] who (like slaves)
had no honour or reputation to lose, whereas affairs with
married women or older men were reprehensible because
they brought discredit on the married woman in the first
case and on the young man himself in the second; for in a
relationship between a boy or youth and an older man it
might be taken for granted that the former had mercenary
motives, was in fact lowering himself to the level of a prosti-
tute. To that extent then, Cicero seems to have felt that love
(=lust) is particularly objectionable in a homosexual form.
But he is not very clear about it and the distinction is not important to him. His quarrel in the *Tusculans* is with *amor*
as such.

On the other hand two passages on the beauty of boys or
youths and those who admire it could hardly have been
written by a determined anti-homosexual:

On duties 1.144:

Pericles was right in what he said to Sophocles, when the latter
was his colleague as General, at a meeting with him on common
business. A beautiful boy happened to go by and Sophocles remarked: 'What a pretty boy, Pericles!' 'A general,' Pericles
replied, 'should keep his eyes from trespassing as well as his hands.'
But if Sophocles had made the same remark during a trial of
athletes, he could not fairly have been blamed. Such is the force of
place and time.

On the nature of the gods 1.79 (the Epicurean spokesman
is speaking):

How few have beauty! When I was in Athens, hardly one per company was to be found with it among the youths. I see you are
smiling, but that's the way it is. Moreover, for those of us who
delight in lads with the permission of the philosophers of old, even
their imperfections are often agreeable. . . . Q. Catulus, father of

---

[13] *Iste qui vulgo appellatur amor* (*Tusc.* iv.68).
[14] Cf. *Cael.* 30, 42.

our colleague and friend, was fond of your fellow-townsman Roscius and wrote these lines to him . . . To Catulus he was more beautiful than a god, yet he had a terrible squint and still has today. But what's the odds, if this very trait seemed piquant and charming to Catulus?

Consideration of Cicero's views on this subject raises a literary problem. About a century and a half after his death, his fervent admirer the younger Pliny answers an enquiry from a correspondent:[15] how was it that the eminently respectable and respectably eminent Pliny composed light and sometimes improper verses? The answer is that it all went back to a certain summer afternoon at Pliny's country house by the sea. He had been listening to a book read aloud after lunch. The writer was Asinius Gallus, whose father, the historian, orator and tragic poet Asinius Pollio was a younger contemporary of Cicero's. Gallus was the author of a monograph comparing the two, naturally in Pollio's favour, in the course of which he quoted an epigram supposedly written by Cicero about his slave (later freedman) and confidential secretary Tiro. Pliny retired to his siesta, but instead of sleep he found a thought, namely that the greatest orators (and to be a great orator was Pliny's most cherished aspiration) had taken pleasure and even pride in turning out such things. In no time at all, even though Pliny was out of versifying practice, that thought resulted in a copy of hexameters:[16]

> When Gallus I read, who pretends that his sire
> Had far more than Tully poetical fire,
> The wisest of men, I perceived, held it fit
> To temper his wisdom with love and with wit;
> For Tully, grave Tully, in amorous strains
> Of the frauds of his paramour Tiro complains,
> That faithless to love and to pleasure untrue,
> From his promis'd embrace the arch wanton withdrew.
> Then said I to my heart, Why shouldst thou conceal
> The sweetest of passions, the love which you feel?
> Yes, fly, wanton Muse, and proclaim it around,
> Thy Pliny has lov'd and his Tiro has found;

[15] Plin. *Epist.* vii.4.
[16] In Melmoth's eighteenth-century translation.

The coy one so artful, who sweetly denies,
And from the soft flame, but to heighten it, flies.

'From this,' continues Pliny, 'I turned to an elegiac poem, which I finished as rapidly; and, swept along[17] by facility, I added other verses.' But the further stages of Pliny's painless ascent of Parnassus are not of present relevance.

Cicero's authorship of the epigram quoted in Gallus' book has generally been discredited. Herr Karl Büchner, in his article on Cicero's letters and fragments in Pauly—Wissowa's encyclopaedia,[18] observes that if Cicero's authorship were accepted, our picture of him would be decisively influenced, whether it were taken as evidence of fact or as a mere frolic. If so, the picture needs retouching. For if Pliny, who had no doubts about the authenticity of the epigram, found no difficulty in accommodating *his* picture of Cicero to its existence, ought *we* to be embarrassed?[19]

Asinius Gallus' book was no doubt hostile to Cicero. The Emperor Claudius composed a reply and Aulus Gellius[20] waxed indignant. But Gellius does not mention the epigram. Gallus may be presumed to have thought it genuine, since he apparently quoted it in a comparison between Cicero and Pollio as poets. He is likely to have found it in a 'Book of (Cicero's) jests' (*iocularis libellus*) from which Quintilian[21] quotes an elegiac couplet. The burden of proof lies upon those who pronounce the epigram spurious, like Herr Büchner, a scholar generally more prone to defend forgeries than to convict them.

---

[17] I read *correptus* for *corruptus*: see a forthcoming note in *Proc. Cam. phil. soc.* 26 (1980).

[18] VII A, 1259f. (1939). This section of the article is entitled 'Gefälschtes Epigramm'.

[19] A discussion by R. Y. Tyrrell, late-Victorian editor of Cicero's correspondence, in the introduction to his first volume—dropped in the third (Tyrrell—Purser) edition—lapses into semi-hysteria. According to this, 'Cicero never speaks but in terms of abhorrence' of 'that crime which it is a shame even to speak of', a statement hardly consistent with passages (*Nat. d.* 1.79, *Off.* 1.144; see above, p. 70) cited in his own footnote. For Tyrrell, Cicero had to abhor homosexuality, just as he had to believe firmly in personal survival after death, never mind what he himself wrote on these matters.

[20] XVII.1.1.

[21] VIII.6.73.

He argues:[22] (1) Such a poem would be uncharacteristic of Cicero's neoteric verse, verse, that is, written in Hellenistic modes, in which he never speaks of himself and always takes his subjects from mythology. This poem, however, like the one from which Quintilian cites, was an epigram, and Hellenistic epigrammatists did not normally take their subjects from mythology. They frequently speak of themselves, and pederasty is part of their stock in trade. (2) The words which Pliny quotes look like later Latin elegy. Which words? Nothing assures us that any particular word in Pliny's poem was taken from the epigram. But one word very well may have been: *savia* ('kisses'). It is found chiefly in Comedy. The only classical example in Lewis—Short's dictionary is from a familiar letter of Cicero's. But Catullus uses the word and its diminutive *saviolum* several times, Horace once in an Epode, Propertius, who affected oddities of vocabulary, twice. It also occurs in a poem of uncertain date and authorship, *Catalepton* 13. By Pliny's time it had been replaced by *basium* and *osculum*; Martial, who has these two by the dozen, never uses *savium*. Probably then Pliny took it from the epigram, which to that extent looks more like a product of Cicero's period than later Latin elegy. (3) In the *Invective against Cicero* attributed to Sallust there is some mockery of Cicero's poetry, and this piece, had the writer known of it, would have been mentioned. Can such things be set down in earnest? Herr Büchner believes that Sallust wrote the *Invective*; I do not. But aside from that, a flimsier *argumentum ex silentio* would be hard to conceive. Add that the *Invective* does not *mock* Cicero's verses; it merely cites two of them to illustrate his arrogance, a charge which would not have been strengthened by the citation of this epigram. (4) Those verse compositions of Cicero which stand close to Hellenistic style are confined to the period before his first visit to Greece, when Tiro was a child or not yet born (I should say definitely not yet born). On the same page Herr Büchner observes that lettered persons in Cicero's time produced epigrams galore.

---

[22] These arguments, essaying to prove that Cicero could not have been the author of the epigram, are formally directed against a fantastic theory of Tyrrell's (not Tyrrell—Purser's) based on the supposition that it is genuine.

It is almost remarkable, he says, that we have only one specimen from Cicero—meaning the one quoted by Quintilian. Clearly there is not the slightest reason why Cicero should not have produced such trifles for his own and his friends' amusement. The collection probably appeared after his death.

The common persuasion that the epigram was spurious is simply a classic example of evidence smothered by emotion. As to Cicero's real relations with Tiro, the epigram has nothing to say. Probably it was no more than what Pliny calls a 'naughty pleasantry', as were presumably Pliny's own efforts in the same line.

It would be ungrateful not to notice a different theory, propounded by Professor W. H. McDermott:[23]

There is now enough information for a conjecture which solves all the problems involved. First, we must picture the scene which inspired the poem. We have suggested above that Tiro was born about 80. Soon after Cicero's return from study in Greece, and before his quaestorship in Sicily, dinner was served at Cicero's home. Tiro, then about three or four years of age, as a favorite in Cicero's *familia*, was brought in to kiss his *dominus*[24] good-night. Children of that age are coy—he refused. A little later, Cicero excused himself from the dining room, went to the boy's bedroom, tucked him in and kissed him. On his return he regaled his guests with a poem on the incident. Later he included it in a small *liber iocularis*. Still later, when Verres saw impending doom, he came upon this poem ... Afterwards, Cicero's friends were much amused at the porcine stupidity of Verres, Sallust unscrupulously followed Verres, later Asinius Gallus fell into Verres' error about the poem, and Dio may well have been similarly misled. This reconstruction is speculative, but highly probable.

To return to the grown-up world, Professor Williams further adduces a passage of Cornelius Nepos[25] listing Greek customs which in Rome would have been considered either infamous or undignified. Among them he mentions that in

---

[23] *Historia* 21 (1972), 274f. In the same paper it is suggested that Tiro was Cicero's son by a concubine.

[24] Evidently the orator is meant, not his father (still living).

[25] Praef. 2–5.

Crete it was creditable to youths to have had lovers, the more the better. That takes us no further. Professor Williams also calls attention to a remark of Quintilian's[26] about the playwright Afranius: 'A pity he sullied his plots with nasty love affairs with boys, thus confessing his own habits.' Quintilian's views, as on corporal punishment in schools, could sometimes be unrepresentative.

Granted that Latin poets of the first century B.C. 'posing as sodomites' follow a Greek convention and that ordinarily inferences as to their personal proclivities and lives should not be drawn: yet if Roman morality, not to speak of the Augustan establishment,[27] had been so sharply averse from all forms of male homosexuality as Professor Williams supposes, this convention would surely not have been tolerated. But Horace's case is exceptional. Professor Williams considers only the Odes. Epode 11 represents him as thoroughly bisexual. More significant, in the early Satire 2 (116f.) he advises those in need of sexual relief not to be fastidious but to take it from any girl *or boy* slave who happens to be handy. In Satires II.3.325 he taxes himself (through Damasippus) with 'a thousand passions for girls, a thousand for boys'. Hellenistic convention is a cock that will not fight in the Satires.

[26] X.1.100.
[27] Maecenas' passion for the actor Bathyllus was notorious.

CHAPTER SEVEN

Epilogue

HORACE's farewell to poetry in Epistles I.I was not to be his last. He repeats it[1] in Epistles II.2, probably the first to be composed of his three long letters about literature: the Letter to Augustus (by special request of the recipient), the Letter to Florus and the 'Art of poetry'—this last addressed not to Maecenas, the mainstay of Horace's poetical career, but to three unidentifiable members of the noble house of Calpurnius Piso. To recall the two 'aspects' of Satires I.4, the 'moral' had indeed taken 'the lion's share' in Horace's *oeuvre*. Even in the Letter to Florus it can be said to take the last seventy-six lines. But the 'artistic' now comes into its own, in a broader, though curiously restricted, perspective. So Horace became the only Latin poet to write at length about poetry. But Horace on poetry is not my theme.

The Letter to Augustus is largely a protest against an alleged public prejudice in favour of the early Latin poets from Ennius and Naevius to Accius to the detriment of contemporaries. 50–60:

> *Ennius et sapiens et fortis et alter Homerus,*   50
> *ut critici dicunt, leviter curare videtur*
> *quo promissa cadant et somnia Pythagorea.*
> *Naevius in manibus non est et mentibus haeret*
> *paene recens? adeo sanctum est vetus omne poema.*
> *ambigitur quoties uter utro sit prior, aufert*   55
> *Pacuvius docti famam senis, Accius alti.*
> *dicitur Afrani toga convenisse Menandro,*
> *Plautus ad exemplar Siculi properare Epicharmi,*

---

[1] The word he uses, *carmina*, may refer only to lyrics.

vincere Caecilius gravitate, Terentius arte.
hos ediscit et hos arto stipata theatro   60
spectat Roma potens.

Wise, brave Ennius, a second Homer as the critics say, is held to
care but little what comes of his promises and Pythagorean dreams.
Is not Naevius in people's hands and does he not hold his place in
their minds as though he were of yesterday? So sacred is every
antique poem. Whenever the respective merits of Pacuvius and
Accius are in question, the former is cried up for a learned ancient,
the latter for a lofty one. Afranius' gown is said to have been a fit
for Menander, Plautus to bustle on the model of Sicilian Epicharmus, Caecilius to take the prize for dignity, Terence for
technique. These mighty Rome learns by rote, these she watches,
packed in a crowded playhouse.

The lines about Ennius (50–2) are problematic. The allusions
to 'promises' and 'Pythagorean dreams' need not be explained here; they amount simply to 'his boast that he will
make a second Homer'. How can he 'be held to care little'
what becomes of that? According to the most favoured interpretation, because, basking in his modern popularity, he
does not have to worry. But how can Ennius, long since in his
grave, 'be held not to worry'? The words are much more
naturally read as a criticism: 'Ennius is held to take little
trouble' to live up to his boast. So indeed they are taken in
Kiessling—Heinze and elsewhere. But the criticism is pa-
tently out of place, as well as inconsistent with *et sapiens et
fortis et alter Homerus*. We need a complimentary judgment
corresponding to those on the other old-time authors who
follow. We need to be told that in the opinion of the public
he *does* (i.e. did) take good care to live up to his boast:

> *Ennius et sapiens et fortis et alter Homerus,*
> *ut critici dicunt, viget et curare videtur*
> *quo promissa cadant*

Ennius . . . is all the rage and held to take good care how his
promises and Pythagorean dreams turn out.

For the use of *vigere* I may refer to my note on a letter of
Cicero to his brother Quintus (III.5.8 (7.1)), where it has
been misunderstood. The Thesaurus (IV.1503.34ff.) provides abundant illustration of *curare* (both positive and

negative) with indirect questions. The scribal bridge from
uigetet to *leuiter* may have been *uitet*.

Horace's complaint against the unfairness of current evalu-
ations of contemporary authors, which is expressly directed
against the general public and not merely the 'critics' of line
51, is best taken with some reservation. If Virgil, Propertius,
Tibullus, and Ovid suffered from public neglect or deprecia-
tion, there is singularly little in their works or elsewhere to
suggest it.[2] I rather suspect that somewhere in the back of
Horace's mind, added to his standing personal preoccupa-
tion with surrounding Envy, was the old issue between
himself and Valerius Cato.[3] But a recent theatrical 'flop' may
have set him off. The Letter to Augustus is much concerned
with drama, the 'Art' almost exclusively.

In the Letter to Florus (41–54) Horace takes a last look at
the way he began:

It was my fortune to be reared in Rome and taught about the
damage which angry Achilles did the Greeks. Kind Athens added
a little finish—made me want to distinguish the straight from the
crooked and search for truth in the woods of Academe. But harsh
times took me away from that pleasant place and the tide of civil
war carried me in my inexperience into ranks which were destined
not to stand against the muscle of Caesar Augustus. Philippi gave
me my discharge. Downcast, my wings clipped, deprived of my
paternal hearth and property, enterprising poverty urged me to
make verses. But now that I have all I need, what quantities of
hemlock will ever suffice to clear my brain were I not to think sleep
a better employment than verse-writing?

Without questioning its veracity, one senses irony in this
selective retrospect. Horace's monument more enduring than
bronze was to outlast the remade Rome of imperial Caesar,
whose magnificently sober record of achievement survives,
however, on stone. It was that Caesar who asked his friends
as he lay dying whether he had played out the farce in
tolerable style. Perhaps he and his 'charming manikin'[4] were
birds of a feather.

---

[2] Not but that occasional complaints of the human tendency to overrate ancients
at the expense of moderns occur elsewhere; see G. Luck on Ov. *Trist.* v.3.55f. But
Horace seems to be making too much of it.

[3] See pp. 3of.   [4] *Homunculus lepidissimus (Vita Horatii).*

Horatiana

Epod. 1.7–14

utrumne iussi persequemur otium,
non dulce ni tecum simul,
an hunc laborem mente laturi, decet
qua ferre non mollis viros?   10
feremus, et te vel per Alpium iuga
inhospitalem et Caucasum
vel Occidentis usque ad ultimum sinum
forti sequemur pectore.

Rereading these lines after a long interval, it struck me that
9–11 should run thus:

an hunc laborem, mente laturi decet
qua ferre non mollis viros,
feremus, et te . . .?

with the question-mark at the end of 14. The point had
already been made by Housman in the first article he published.[1] But, to adapt a saying of his own, who was Housman
that editors should pay attention to him?

Epod. 5.55–70

formidolosis dum latent silvis ferae   55
dulci sopore languidae,
senem, quod omnes rideant, adulterum
latrent Suburanae canes
nardo perunctum, quale non perfectius
meae laborarint manus.   60

---

[1] 'Horatiana', *Journ. phil.* 10 (1882), 187–96 = *Classical papers*, pp. 1–8.

> *quid accidit? cur dira barbarae minus*
>   *venena Medeae valent? . . .*
> *atqui nec herba nec latens in asperis*   67
>   *radix fefellit me locis.*
> indormit *unctis omnium cubilibus*
>   *oblivione paelicum.*   70
> *a! a! solutus ambulat veneficae*
>   *scientioris carmine.*

latrant[2] should be read in 57. Canidia is stating the outrageous fact; a wish or imprecation is out of place, even if
there were any obvious reason why she should want the dogs
to bark. In 69 the text contradicts what precedes. The old
fellow cannot be gadding about town while obliviously asleep
in a drugged bed. 69f. present an alternative. Was he safe at
home after all?

> *an dormit unctis omnium cubilibus*
>   *oblivione paelicum?*

Epod. 9.1–6

> *Quando repostum Caecubum ad festas dapes*
>   *victore laetus Caesare*
> *tecum sub alta,* sic *Iovi gratum, domo*
>   *beate Maecenas, bibam*
> *sonante mixtum tibiis carmen lyra,*
>   *hac Dorium, illis barbarum?*

Should not the obscure *sic Iovi gratum*, as Wistrand rightly
called it, be replaced by *si Iovi gratum*, equivalent to 'D. V.'?
Cf. Ter. *Eun.* 919f. *si dis placet,/spero me habere qui hunc meo
excruciam modo* (see, however, Fraenkel, *Kl. Beiträge*, II, p. 63),
Ov. *Met.* IV. 701f. *addere tantis/dotibus et meritum, faveant modo
numina, tempto* (also Pers. 5.113f. *esto/liberque ac sapiens praetoribus
ac Iove dextro*).

---

[2] Housman was first with this correction, though others proposed it later independently (see note in Campbell's edition) and it might be expected to occur to
any attentive reader.

Sat. I.1.108–112

> *illuc unde abii redeo :* nemon, ut *avarus,*
> *se probet ac potius laudet diversa sequentis?*
> *quodque aliena capella gerat distentius uber*   110
> *tabescat? neque se maiori pauperiorum*
> *turbae comparet? hunc atque hunc superare laboret?*

So Rudd, to whose lengthy discussion[3] I refer. He translates:[4]

I return to my starting point: is no one, because of his greed, to be content with his own situation, and is every man to envy, instead, those pursuing other ways of life? Because his neighbour's goat carries a more bulging udder is he to be consumed with jealousy...?

But to take *ut avarus* as *utpote avarus* ('because of his greed') is as desperate a course as any. Who would write *nemon, ut avarus, se probet?* when he meant *omnes, ut avari, se improbent??* And why the questions? We want statements. To Fraenkel[5] the solution seemed so simple that 'one blushes to put it down': *nemon ut avarus se probet?* is a 'repudiating question'. Linguistically that is unexceptionable, but Fraenkel was quite right to blush, for the question is fatuous: 'What, no greedy man like himself? The very idea!' Instead of these extremities, change a letter, *n* to *ē* (=*est*). *nemo est ut avarus se probet*='there is no way that any greedy man should like himself'. The *est ut* construction is used twice elsewhere by Horace, in *Odes* III.1.9f. *est ut viro vir latius ordinet/arbusta sulcis* and *Epist.* 1.1.12f. *non est ut copia maior/ab Iove donari possit tibi.* At the start of the Satire Horace says that *nobody* is content with his lot. But having shown to his own satisfaction that discontent is due to greed, he does not have to maintain that exaggeration. Where there is no greed, there is no discontent —a rare phenomenon but not unknown (117–19):

> *inde fit ut raro, qui se vixisse beatum*
> *dicat et exacto contentus tempore vita*
> *cedat uti conviva satur, reperire queamus.*

---

[3] Pp. 274f.   [4] Pp. 13f.   [5] Pp. 97–101.

Sat. 1.2.77–82

> *quare, ne paeniteat te,*
> *desine matronas sectarier, unde laboris*
> *plus haurire mali est quam ex re decerpere fructus.*
> *nec magis huic inter niveos viridisque lapillos*   80
> *(sit licet hoc, Cerinthe, tuum) tenerum est femur aut crus*
> *rectius, atque etiam melius persaepe togatae est.*

So e.g. Lejay (without *est* in 82), following Lambinus' interpretation of the parenthesis: 'licet haec tua stultitia est ut
ames divites matronas.' *hoc* cannot be taken so, and a reference to Cerinthus as another adulterer, whether or not
identical with the person addressed in the previous sentence,
is pointless. *hoc* can only refer to *niveos viridesque lapillos* (cf.
Kühner—Stegmann, *Lat. gramm.* 1, 61f.): 'even though this
(the jewellery) be Cerinthus' work.' Cerinthus I take to have
been a Cellini or Fabergé of contemporary fame.

Otherwise Fraenkel,[6] who takes *hoc* with Gesner as ablative
(=*ideo*) and reads *tuo* with Bentley, thus arriving at the para-
phrase: 'nec huic matronae, licet sit inter niveos et virides
lapillos, ideo femur aut crus magis tenerum est quam tuum,
o Cerinthe' (he means 'femur magis tenerum aut crus
rectius'). That position had been demolished by Housman
'in a juvenile paper'[7] with two arguments; Fraenkel mis-
understands the first and ignores the second. Housman's first
objection was, not that Cerinthus is 'dragged in' (like Catia
in line 95), but that he gets in the way of the comparison
between *matrona* and *togata*:

> The question in hand is the relative desirability of the *matrona* and
> the *togata*; and if reason is to hold her seat 'magis tenerum' must
> mean 'magis tenerum quam togatae'.

If only Fraenkel had 'paused to observe' what an im-
measurably superior critic[8] was really saying, he could have
spared himself the trouble of illustrating 'a certain peculiarity

---

[6] Pp. 84–6.

[7] *Journ. phil.* 18 (1890), 1f. = *Classical papers*, pp. 136f. Housman was born in 1859.

[8] I do not say 'scholar'. Fraenkel's book will be admired for its learning and enjoyed for its vitality so long as interest in its subject survives.

of Horace's early satires', namely his practice of striking 'a swift blow at this or that individual, in passing as it were.'

Housman's second argument is equally incontrovertible and even more difficult to misunderstand:

This reading supposes Cerinthus to be, as Porphyrion says he was, a '*prostibulum insignis speciei atque candoris*': well then, *femur Cerinthi* will be *tenerrimum*, *crus Cerinthi* will be *rectissimum*; so it becomes not only pointless but senseless to say, by way of disparaging matrons, that *femur matronae* is not *magis tenerum*, that *crus matronae* is not *rectius*.

Sat. 1.3.30–2

> rideri possit eo quod
> rusticius tonso toga defluit et male laxus
> in pede calceus haeret.

Since *rusticius* has to be taken with *tonso*, *toga defluit* stands on its own. What was inelegant about a toga flowing down? In Macrobius (*Saturn.* III.13.4) the well-dressed Roman arranges his toga so as to envelop the body *as it flows down: togam corpori sic applicabat ut . . . sinus ex composito defluens modum lateris ambiret*. If Horace had meant 'flowed down to his ankles' or the like, as in Virgil (*Aen.* 1.404) *pedes vestis defluxit ad imos*, ought he not to have said so? I rather think he wrote *diffluit*. The toga, like the shoe, is a loose fit and billows out as the man walks. When Cicero speaks of Catiline's young following wearing togas 'like sails' (*Catil.* 2.22; cf. *Epod.* 4.8),[9] he is talking of dandies, not hobbledehoys, but what the dandy does in calculated defiance of the norm[10] the hobbledehoy may do out of ignorance or carelessness.

---

[9] See also A. A. R. Henderson on Ov. *Rem. am.* 679f.

[10] I think it quite possible that Macrobius too wrote *diffluens*, in which case the operative words are *ex composito*.

Sat. II.6.29–31

> '*quid tibi vis, insane, et* quam rem agis?' *improbus* urget
> *iratis* precibus. '*tu pulses omne quod obstat,*   30
> *ad Maecenatem memori si mente recurras.*'

So Kiessling—Heinze, following Bentley's conjecture in 29.
The manuscript tradition is unmetrical: *quid tibi vis, insane,
et quas res agis?* No reading can be sound which makes *improbus* ('outrageous', 'unconscionable') apply, not to Horace,
to whose behaviour it is fully appropriate, but to his innocent
victim. Add that *precibus* is ambiguous; it might mean either
'pleas' or 'curses', for the words attributed to the *improbus* are
neither the one nor the other. I have translated:

> '*quid tibi vis, insane, et quas res [agis] improbus urges*
> *iratis pedibus? tu pulses omne quod obstat,*
> *ad Maecenatem memori si mente recurras?*'

Cf. *Sat.* II.7.6f. *pars hominum vitiis gaudet constanter et urget/
propositum,* and for *iratis pedibus Sat.* II.8.5 *iratum ventrem,* Prop.
III.25.10 *nec tamen irata ianua fracta manu,* Ov. *Met.* IV.100
timido pede fugit in antrum et sim. *tu . . . recurras* is best taken as
a 'repudiating question'.

Sat. II.7.61f.

>   *estne marito*
> *matronae peccantis in ambo iusta potestas?*
> *in corruptorem vel iustior. illa tamen se*
> *non habitu mutatve loco peccatve superne,*
> *cum te formidet mulier neque credat amanti.*   65

Lejay's note will serve as well as any to make visible the
darkness of 64f.:

La suite est obscure. 'Elle n'a pas la responsabilité supérieure de la
faute, puisque, étant femme, elle te redoute' (Havet). Mais *superne*
a, dans les passages connus, un sense matériel (*A.p.* 4 *mulier formosa
superne . . .*). Les éditeurs modernes . . . rapprochent le v. 50
(*supinum*). Le sens général paraît être: 'La femme du monde est

passive'. Puis, vient une idée à demi sous-entendue, comme souvent: 'Elle ne cède même que parce qu'elle te redoute.'

Now even if *non peccat superne* could be a way of saying οὐ κελητίζει (which I rather doubt) and even if it were true that 'la femme du monde est passive' (for which I know no evidence), the statement is alien to Davus' point, which is that the male partner in adultery deserves punishment more than the female. When all is said and done (*tamen*), *she* does not leave her house disguised as a slave, as he does (53–6). *neque peccat superne* implies that the lover does just that, which is silly. The senseless *superne* must have replaced another word. That word may (I hesitate to say 'must', though I doubt whether there is any alternative) have been *pudice*. Some lines of Propertius (II.23.13–22) are relevant:

> *contra, reiecto quae libera vadit amictu*
> *custodum et nullo saepta timore placet . . .*
> *nec dicet 'timeo, propera iam surgere, quaeso:*
> *infelix, hodie vir mihi rure venit.'*   20
> *et quas Euphrates et quas mihi misit Orontes*
> *me iuverint: nolim furta pudica tori.*

The married lady commits adultery 'modestly': *peccatque pudice. pudice* having accidentally dropped out someone was inspired by 50, *clunibus aut agitavit equum lasciva supinum* to give the line an ending with *peccatve superne*.

That still leaves the problem of 65, which is foolish, whatever we make of 64. For why in a sane world would Davus assume that the *matrona* is afraid of her *lover*? It does not help in the least to take 65 with what follows. The otiose *mulier* smells of an interpolator. He felt, reasonably enough, that *peccatve superne* needed explanation and found one which, foolish as it was, has satisfied most editors—that the lady did not trust her lover enough to engage in such improprieties.

Sat. *II.8.18*

In Fundanius' narrative of Nasidienus' comic dinner-party, the rich-vulgarian host provides Caecuban and Chian wines, but says to Maecenas: 'If you prefer Alban or Falernian to what's in front of you, we have both.' Horace sarcastically interjects: *divitias miseras!* ('The sorrows of the rich!'). On this Rudd:[11]

There has been much dispute about this phrase, but it certainly need not imply stinginess on Nasidienus' part. Probably it is just a vague expression referring sarcastically to his foolish ostentation. If, however, we want to examine it more closely, we may start from the remark of Ofellus in II.2.65–6:

> mundus erit qua non offendat sordibus, atque
> in neutram partem cultus miser.

(The wise man) will be stylish enough to avoid giving offence through meanness, and in his way of living he will not be unhappy in either direction (i.e. towards meanness *or* extravagance).

When a man's conduct misses or exceeds the appropriate mean he fails to achieve happiness and becomes to that extent *miser*. He may be unaware of this himself; he may not *feel* unhappy. But the fact that others view him with dislike or contempt is an index of his true condition. 'So-and-so's a miserable character', we say. By a slight extension the adjective can then be applied to the cause of the man's condition, as in *misera ambitione* (1.4.26). In Nasidienus' case it is lavish ostentation which makes him an object of ridicule; hence riches are *miserae*, 'unhappy'—a striking way to speak of something which is supposed to make a man *beatus*. And one remembers that in the first line Nasidienus *is* called *beatus*.

I believe the answer to be more straightforward, 'so simple that one blushes to put it down'. Horace is ironically compassionating Nasidienus' desperate anxiety to please, as does one of the guests in 67–70:

Just fancy! There you go, tormenting yourself so as to give me slap-up hospitality, harrassed by all manner of anxieties—is the bread scorched, is the sauce badly seasoned, are the servants properly dressed and groomed?

If Nasidienus had not been a wealthy man, he would have been spared the misery of worrying which wines would best please his distinguished guest. *cur valle permutem Sabina/*

---

[11] Pp. 217f.

divitias operosiores? And, after all, Gesner had read the riddle:
'*quae sic sollicitum habeant dominum, quem copia incertum faciat.*'

Sat. II.8.25–33

Nomentanus ad hoc, qui, si quid forte lateret, 25
indice monstraret digito: nam cetera turba,
nos, inquam, cenamus aves, conchylia, pisces
longe dissimilem noto celantia sucum,
ut vel continuo patuit, cum passeris atque
ingustata mihi porrexerat ilia rhombi. 30
post hoc me docuit melimela rubere minorem
ad lunam delecta. quid hoc intersit ab ipso
audieris melius.

Nomentanus had been invited as a connoisseur and assigned
the place normally occupied by the host, *summus in imo*, so
that he could point out items which might otherwise have
been overlooked to his neighbour Maecenas and to other
guests.

Lines 27f. are generally held to mean that the natural
flavour of the viands was disguised by sauces, etc. That
would hardly have been a novelty to Maecenas and his
friends. Now as Rudd observes,[12] *ingustata mihi* cannot with
this interpretation be understood 'which I had never tasted
before.' So 'by *ingustata* Fundanius means that during the
meal no one had yet tasted this particular preparation; he
was the first to discover its surprising flavour.' That is unsatisfactory in several ways: (1) The information that the
dish had not yet been tasted by anybody is beside the point
and might have been left to be taken for granted after *vel
continuo.* (2) Why should Horace choose something so re-
cherché as *ilia passeris atque rhombi* to illustrate the disguising
of the flavours? Something quite ordinary, a chicken say,
would have been the natural choice. (3) *mihi* is naturally
taken with *ingustata* as well as *porrexerat.* (4) The information
which follows about apples picked at the waning of the
moon has nothing to do with concealment of flavour. Such

[12] P. 218.

apples, so Nomentanus will have claimed, had a distinctive flavour which would probably be unfamiliar to the guests.

longe dissimilem noto is therefore better understood as 'far different from any known to us'; different, that is, either because the items were unusual in themselves, like the *ilia*, or because of some special quality, as with the apples.

Sat. *II.8.90–5*

> tum pectore adusto 90
> vidimus et merulas poni et sine clune palumbes,
> suavis res, si non causas narraret earum et
> naturas dominus; quem nos sic fugimus ulti,
> ut nihil omnino gustaremus, velut illis
> Canidia adflasset peior serpentibus Afris. 95

At the end of this satire Fundanius, Maecenas and the others rush out of the house leaving the latter part of the meal untouched. Structurally it is the weakest ending in the book, and (however fictitious in content) it puts the guests in an exceedingly poor light —to our way of thinking. But this cannot have been Horace's intention, for the piece, like 1.9, was written for the entertainment of these very people. He must have seen their departure as a dramatic gesture which paid the host back for his absurd and vulgar display.

So Rudd.[13] His misconception is not universal (Kiessling— Heinze's note is sound), but worth signalising in justice to Roman manners. What Fundanius says is that, after they had declined to eat any more (they had already had boar, birds, shellfish, fish among other things), they 'escaped' from their host, i.e. took their leave. That they did so sooner than they decently could is not fairly to be inferred.

Incidentally, the somewhat abrupt ending is characteristic of narrative satire, as 1.5, 1.9, and Seneca's *Apocolocyntosis*.

---

[13] P. 222.

Odes 1.14.18f (O navis, referent)

nuper sollicitum quae mihi taedium,
nunc desiderium curaque non levis

These lines are rightly claimed by Fraenkel and Nisbet—
Hubbard to prove that the ship of this ode must be alle-
gorical, and they hold with Quintilian that she is the Ship of
State. Against which W. S. Anderson[14] urges among other
things that

> you cannot miss your own state, because you sail aboard it and you
> must sink with it; it is by definition part of you.

A point well taken. Kiessling—Heinze's explanation that
desiderium means 'yearning for its tranquil possession'
stretches the sense unduly; and why should such a feeling
have developed only 'now'? Nisbet—Hubbard have a different way out: 'Horace is ἐραστὴς τῆς πόλεως (cf. Thuc.
II.43.1)', for '*desiderium* does not necessarily imply that the
loved one is absent or hard to win'. But does it not? It may
indeed refer to *past* longing (here ruled out by *nunc*), as in
Petron. 139.4 *teneo te, inquit, qualem speraveram, tu desiderium
meum, tu voluptas mea,* but can it be simply an alias for *amor*? I
think not. The Ship of State also runs into chronological
shoals. None of the composition dates canvassed in Nisbet—
Hubbard's note is very plausible. As for Alcaeus, Anderson
has shown that he settles nothing.

But for the untoward intrusion of the Ship of State, readers
might legitimately gather that the ship represents a beloved
person. This person had caused Horace much worry and
heartache in the not distant past. Now he or she is in grave
danger. Horace can only look on from a distance, wishing he
were on the spot and deeply concerned. That is all he has
seen fit to tell us. Do we really need any more?

[14] *Cl. phil.* 61 (1966), 88.

Odes 1.20.1–8

Vile potabis modicis Sabinum
cantharis, Graeca quod ego ipse testa
conditum levi, datus in theatro
  cum tibi plausus,

care, Maecenas, eques, ut paterni   5
fluminis ripae simul et iocosa
redderet laudes tibi Vaticani
  montis imago.

clare, advocated by Bentley, is widely accepted and probably right, but since *care* is the tradition, what can be said on its behalf deserves saying. Taken as 'dear (to me)' it will not do (see Nisbet—Hubbard). But suppose it means 'dear (to others)', as in II.17.7f. *nec carus aeque nec superstes/integer* on which again see Nisbet—Hubbard. Then we could understand: 'Knight as you are [Knights being generally not conspicuous enough to be greeted with applause in the theatre], Rome loves you.' *care* will allude to the applause, *eques* to Maecenas' entry as he took his place in the fourteen rows behind the Senators. Nisbet—Hubbard's statement that *clarus* is a word normally reserved for Senators could mislead. The simple adjective is not ordinarily so used, though *clarissimus* is, but only of particularly distinguished Senators.

Odes 1.25.9f (Parcius iunctas)

invicem moechos anus arrogantis
flebis in solo levis angiportu

'*moechos arrogantis* sc. *esse*', Kiessling—Heinze, explaining that this is the substance, not the cause, of Lydia's complaint. I prefer to take *moechos* as direct object: 'You shall bewail your (now) arrogant lovers', i.e. bewail their absence or loss. Cf. III.7.1–5 *quid fles, Asterie, . . . Gygen?*

Odes 1.35.21–4 (O diva, gratum)

> te Spes et albo rara Fides colit
> velata panno nec comitem abnegat
> utcumque mutata potentis
> veste domos inimica linquis.

This text absolutely defies understanding. Throughout the
rest of this hymn to Fortune she is the power that controls all
human destinies. Here *te* (as the text stands) has to be the
Fortune (or rather Fortunes) of particular individuals or
families, on which see Nisbet—Hubbard's note. But *inimica*,
as they say,

introduces the most extraordinary confusion . . . Fortune is now a
deity independent of the house, who has gone off and left the great
man in the lurch . . . In such contexts the faithful friend ought to
be praised precisely because he does *not* accompany Fortune; cf.
Ov. *Pont.* 2.3.55f. 'indignum . . . ducis/te fieri comitem stantis in
orbe deae' [and two other passages].

A. Y. Campbell proposed *manicata* ('in chains'). 'One
would rather try *lacrimosa* or something of the kind.' But no
such counsels of despair are worth considering, because we
should still be left with one kind of Fortune in this stanza and
another in the other nine. And can Hope and Loyalty be
envisaged as following the great man's Fortune while he
himself is 'left in the lurch'?
There is but one solution: to read *sed* (Peerlkamp, ap-
proved though not adopted by Lucian Müller) for *nec*, thus
removing all difficulty, though not for Nisbet—Hubbard,
who think that *mutata veste* then has to be applied not to
Fortuna but to *potentis domos* 'and this is not an obvious way of
reading the passage' (no way at all, I should say). They
assume that *mutata veste*, which they translate 'in mourning',
implies sympathy on Fortune's part. That need not be so.
Since Fortune has become malefic, she naturally goes into
black, the proper colour for sinister creatures like Aeschylus'
Furies (*Eum.* 370 ἀμετέραις ἐφόδοις μελανείμοσιν). Their further objection that 'it seems more natural to praise Fides for
accompanying the deity she escorts than for a refusal to

accompany her' seems to me insubstantial as an argument
against the correction; their own note, cited above, goes a
long way to refute it. But a copyist's feeling that Faith should
accompany rather than refuse to accompany accounts for
the error. Housman, on Manil. 3.312, remarks that
although *sed* and *nec* do not look much alike, copyists quite
often confuse them (with examples).

Odes *II.12.21–4 (Nolis longa)*

num tu, quae tenuit dives Achaemenes
aut pinguis Phrygiae Mygdonias opes
permutare velis crine Licymniae,
    plenas aut Arabum domos?

The scholiast's identification of Licymnia with Maecenas'
wife Terentia has been lent more credence than it deserves.
Truly, as Nisbet—Hubbard say, the question *num tu . . .
velis?* is naturally interpreted 'If *you* were as lucky as I am,
would you . . .?' (cf. Cic. *ad Att.* IV.19.2 *hunc tu non ames?*). On
the other hand, to ask a middle-aged husband whether he
would exchange his adored young wife for money is offensive
and inept, even though *num* expects the answer 'no' and the
question is enveloped in hyperbole. The fact that Maecenas
was already enormously wealthy makes matters no better.

Odes *III.1.33–40 (Odi profanum)*

contracta pisces aequora sentiunt
iactis in altum molibus; huc frequens
    caementa demittit redemptor
        cum famulis *dominusque terrae*   35

fastidiosus: sed Timor et Minae
scandunt eodem quo dominus, neque
    decedit aerata triremi et
        post equitem sedet atra Cura.   40

huc . . . fastidiosus is generally understood to mean that many
contractors, along with their workmen, and owners let down

foundations into the sea. But why mention the workmen?
And why bring in the owners at *this* point? Certainly these
may be said to let down foundations in the sense that they
give the orders, but then *redemptor cum famulis* is *de trop.*[15]
Moreover, when *dominus* and *famuli* are found together, it is
natural to assume that the latter belong to the former. The
Thesaurus s.v. *famulus* (*-la*) supplies Accius, frag. 3.6 *ut cum
dominis famuli epulentur ibidem,* Cic. *Leg.* II.27 *cum dominis, tum
famulis,* Catull. 63.51f. *dominos ut erifugae/famuli solent,* Luc.
II.148f. *domini per viscera ferrum/exegit famulus,* Colum. VII.12.1
quis famulus amantior domini?, Ov. *Met.* IV.5 *famulas dominasque*
(add ibid. VIII.635 *nec refert dominos illic famulosne requiras*).

> *huc frequens*
> *caementa demittit redemptor.*
> *tum famuli dominusque terrae*
>
> *fastidiosus sed Timor et Minae*
> *scandunt eodem quo dominus . . .*

I.e. *tum famuli dominusque (scandunt) sed eodem quo dominus
(scandit) scandunt Timor et Minae.* When the building is ready,
the servants and then the master move in, but so do Fear and
Threats. The verb *scandunt* (ἀπὸ κοινοῦ; cf. *Odes* 1.36.5–7 *caris
multa sodalibus,/nulli plura tamen dividit oscula/quam dulci
Lamiae*) pictures them as climbing on board a ship; cf.
II.16.21f. *scandit aeratas vitiosa navis/Cura.*

Odes III.9

> *Donec gratus eram tibi*
> *nec quisquam potior bracchia candidae*
> *cervici iuvenis dabat,*
> *Persarum vigui rege beatior.*

---

[15] From Campbell's note: 'It is, of course, nothing short of grotesque thus to link
the *dominus* with the *redemptor* (*cum famulis*) as one who joins with him (and them) in
the process *caementa demittit* . . . Mueller's parody of this sentence is worth a page
of argument: *praefectus cum fabris et Caesar in Rheno pontem fecit.*'

'*donec non alia magis*   5
arsisti neque erat Lydia post Chloen,
multi Lydia nominis
Romana vigui clarior Ilia.'

me nunc Thressa Chloe regit,
dulces docta modos et citharae sciens,   10
pro qua non metuam mori,
si parcent animae fata superstiti.

'*me torret face mutua*
Thurini Calais filius Ornyti,
pro quo bis patiar mori,   15
si parcent puero fata superstiti.'

quid si prisca redit Venus
diductosque iugo cogit aeneo?
si flava excutitur Chloe,
reiectaeque *patet ianua Lydiae?*   20

'*quamquam sidere pulchrior*
ille est, tu levior cortice et improbo
iracundior Hadria,
tecum vivere amem, tecum obeam libens.'

As some modern editors realise, *reiectae Lydiae* in line 20
must be dative, not genitive, but the ambiguity is awkward
enough. A somewhat less obvious objection to the text is that
the fifth stanza upsets the balance between the two partners
in the dialogue so carefully maintained in the two preceding
stanza-pairs. It makes Horace the breaker of the original
relationship, who now condescendingly opens his door to the
rejected one. The sixth stanza could have redressed the scale,
but does not.

Read *reiectoque*. Horace will throw out Chloe, whom he
has put in Lydia's place; Lydia on her side will open the
door from which she had once driven Horace away.

Odes *III.17.1–10*

Aeli, vetusto nobilis ab Lamo—
quando et priores hinc Lamias ferunt
denominatos et nepotum
per memores genus omne fastos,

auctore ab illo ducis *originem*   5
qui Formiarum moenia dicitur
princeps et innantem Maricae
litoribus tenuisse Lirim

late tyrannus— : cras foliis nemus sqq.   10

So punctuated in Kiessling—Heinze and elsewhere. Horace's
Lamia was the son of a Roman Knight who became Praetor
under Caesar; he himself became Consul twenty years after
the publication of the Odes. Thus *per memores fastos* as applied to his *ancestors* is an unseemly hyperbole. Furthermore,
nepotum naturally refers to *his* descendants, not theirs. The
excision of 2–5 was one way of putting matters straight.
Another is to read *ducet* (D. Heinsius' *ducit*, advocated by
Bentley and accepted by some editors, was a step in the right
direction) in 5 and repunctuate:

Aeli, vetusto nobilis ab Lamo,
quando et priores hinc Lamias ferunt
denominatos et nepotum
per memores genus omne fastos

auctore ab illo ducet originem,   5
qui sqq.

A prophecy of future greatness for the family; and like another of Horace's prophecies (*Odes* II.17.1–16), it came true.

Odes III.19.1–8

Quantum distet ab Inacho
Codrus pro patria non timidus mori,
 narras et genus Aeaci
et pugnata sacro bella sub Ilio :

 quo Chium pretio cadum   5
mercemur, quis aquam temperet ignibus,
 quo praebente domum et quota
Paelignis caream frigoribus, taces.

These opening stanzas show Horace wondering where he is going to get a night's lodging. *quis aquam temperet ignibus* in conjunction with *quo praebente domum* (with which cf. *Sat.* 1.5.38 *Murena praebente domum, Capitone culinam*) has nothing to do with hot drinks, it means 'who is to heat water for a bath', a natural concomitant. Cicero writes to a prospective host (*Ad fam.* IX.16.9) *ego tibi unum sumptum adferam, quod balneum calfacias oportebit* and to a prospective guest (*Ad Att.* II.3.4) *tu prid. Compitalia memento. balneum calfieri iubebo.*

The remaining five stanzas show the poet spending an evening in riotous company. The notion that the first two envisage a 'Dutch treat', and that this is it, should be swept into the rubbish-heap. Only one scenario will fit. As in *Sat.* 1.5, Horace is travelling, in company with the person addressed. Since he refers to the Paelignian frosts, they are travelling in that part of Italy, presumably in winter. Looking to the next stage of their journey, they will need to buy wine and to fix on a place to stay the following night. *quota (hora)* in effect = 'how long will it take me to get there?'

Where are they now? 21–8:

 parcentes ego dexteras
odi : sparge rosas ; audiat invidus
 dementem strepitum Lycus
et vicina seni non habilis Lyco.

 spissa te nitidum coma,   25
puro te similem, Telephe, Vespero
 tempestiva petit Rhode :
me lentus Glycerae torret amor meae.

Evidently the party is taking place in a town, perhaps in the travellers' lodgings. Local acquaintance is implied. There is a young lady living within earshot with a disagreeable old husband, and she is in love with Telephus, one of the drinkers. Horace thinks of his own mistress back in Rome.

Although an opening address to a person not named later in the poem seems to be unique,[16] it looks as though it has to be accepted here. The tedious antiquary of the first stanza can hardly be the handsome young spark of the last.

Odes III.27.13f. (*Impium parrae*)

sis licet felix ubicumque mavis
et memor nostri, Galatea, vivas.

sis licet (sc. *per me*) *felix* is odd, especially as *licet* does not govern *vivas*. For *licet=utinam* is not Latin, though scholars behave as if it was at Ov. *Met.* III.405 *sic amet ipse licet, sic non potiatur amato*. There we should understand 'it could be that *he* will fall in love as I have done', which in the context does indeed amount to a wish, just as 'you may be sorry one day' implies that this is what the speaker hopes will happen. Better, as preferred by T. E. Page in his note though not in his text:

sis (licet) felix ubicumque sqq.

'May you be happy (yes, it's all right) wherever you prefer and may you live . . .'

Odes IV.7.21–8 (*Diffugere nives*)

cum semel occideris et de te splendida Minos
fecerit arbitria,
non, Torquate, genus, non te facundia, non te
restituet pietas.

---

[16] II.5 is probably a soliloquy; see Nisbet—Hubbard.

infernis neque enim tenebris Diana pudicum   25
        liberat Hippolytum,
nec Lethaea valet Theseus abrumpere caro
        vincula Pirithoo.

Since Wilamowitz's breezy dismissal of *Odes* I.4 (*Solvitur acris hiems*) and IV.7 as 'two trivial spring songs', their actual and respective merits have been the occasion of some scholarly skirmishing. Reacting against Housman's 'inarticulate adulation' of *Diffugere nives*, N. E. Collinge[17] complains among other things of a 'maladroit use of mythology', in that according to alternative versions of the legends both Hippolytus and Pirithous *were* rescued. That is hard on Horace, who may rather be supposed to have chosen these two out of all Hades precisely because those versions existed (why else after all?): *no one* has escaped, not even Hippolytus or Pirithous (despite some reports to the contrary). Neither in my opinion is the epithet *splendida* in 21 to be deprecated as 'purely ornamental'. Horace, *verbis felicissime audax*,[18] expected his readers to use a little imagination. When I come to enter Minos' courtroom, I look for it and him to *gleam*, in jet, gold (not forgetting the Homeric sceptre),[19] and scarlet.

Epist. 1.4.6–11

        di tibi formam,
di tibi divitias dederunt artemque fruendi.
quid voveat dulci nutricula maius alumno
qui sapere et fari possit quae sentiat et cui
gratia, fama, valetudo contingat abunde   10
et mundus victus non deficiente crumina?

Bentley construes: *alumno qui possit sapere . . . quid maius voveat nutricula?* But has not Horace just answered that ques-

---

[17] *The structure of Horace's Odes* (1961), p. 111. Similarly A. J. Woodman in his article on this ode (a remarkable essay in the genial art of reducing poetry to sawdust) in *Latomus* 31 (1972): 'He seems to be guilty of an unthinking allusion here' (p. 765). For La Penna *Diffugere nives* remains 'senza dubbio la regina delle odi oraziane' (p. lxxxi).

[18] Quint. X.1.96.   [19] *Od.* XI.569.

tion? Better, I think: *quid maius* (sc. *quam artem fruendi*) *voveat nutricula alumno qui possit sapere* sqq.

Epist. 1.9.1–4

Septimius, Claudi, nimirum intellegit unus
quanti me facias; nam cum rogat et prece cogit
scilicet ut tibi se laudare et tradere coner,
dignum mente domoque legentis honesta Neronis . . .

Line 4 is a metrical monstrosity. Horace must have known that, so what effect did he intend? According to Kiessling— Heinze, following Orelli, he wished to convey the impression of careless writing, so that the praise of the Emperor's stepson seems to slip out unawares. But Horace would not wish to convey the impression of writing carelessly to the Emperor's stepson. No more happy, as it seems to me, are the explanations of two nineteenth-century German editors, H. Schütz and Lucian Müller. The former thought the apparent carelessness was perhaps designed to make the language sound more like prose. The latter saw an admirable representation of Tiberius' nature, 'vorsichtige, verschlossene, zähe, und kälte'! To me the rhythm suggest Septimius' boring, plodding, style. This is what he wants Horace to say about him (*dignum* = ὡς ἄξιον).

In lines 10f. of the same letter,

sic ego maioris fugiens opprobria culpae
frontis ad urbanae descendi praemia,

The meaning of *praemia* is disputed. I think it is best to take it as = *palmam* ('the prize for impudence'), despite the parallel expression in *Odes* 1.1.29 *doctarum hederae praemia frontium*, where 'prerogative' or 'perquisite' suits best, as in *Sat.*1.5.35 *insani ridentes praemia scribae. descendi* corresponds to κατέβην in the sense of εἰς ἀγῶνα καταβῆναι, an observation which I owe to Hugh Lloyd-Jones.

Epist. 1.15.10–13

> mutandus locus est et deversoria nota   10
> praeteragendus equus. 'quo tendis? non mihi Cumas
> est iter aut Baias', laeva stomachosus habena
> dicet eques; sed equi frenato est auris in ore.

The rider tugs at the left-hand rein to stop his horse taking the customary right turn leading to the coast. *laeva stoma-chosus habena*, taken together, has to be understood 'angry by reason of the left rein', out of which interpreters extract 'angrily tugging at the left rein'. The only visible alternative to this imperious exegesis is to take *laeva habena* with *dicet*: 'he will say with his left rein.' So F. G. Doering in his edition of 1831: 'non verbis, sed *habena* sinistrorsum equum flectente dicam, non audit enim equus.' H. Schütz and J. Préaux follow him. That leaves the problem of *sed* which is the wrong particle either way, as Lucian Müller saw and as Kiessling—Heinze's edition recognises in a note which is at odds with their text, making *sed . . . est* part of the rider's speech. One toys with *nam equi*; the metrical irregularity (cf. *Sat.* 2.2.28, 1.9.38) could have prompted the substitution.

Epist. 1.17.35–42

> principibus placuisse viris non ultima laus est.   35
> 'non cuivis homini contingit adire Corinthum.'
> sedit, qui timuit ne non succederet. 'esto.
> quid qui pervenit, fecitne viriliter?' atqui
> hic est aut numquam quod quaerimus. hic onus horret,
> ut parvis animis et parvo corpore maius;   40
> hic subit et perfert. aut virtus nomen inane est
> aut decus et pretium recte petit experiens vir.

The question *fecitne viriliter?*, inane whether *ne = nonne* or not, disrupts the dialogue:

'To have found favour with leading men is something to a person's credit.'

'Not everyone makes it to Corinth.'

'True, there are those who sit at home, afraid of failure.'

'All right, but what about someone who actually gets there and plays the man? (Is he in clover)'[20]

'Ah, but that (playing the man) is the name of the game. Enterprise is better than cowardice, any road.'

Read *fecitque.*

Epist. 1.18.10–14

> alter in obsequium plus aequo pronus et imi   10
> derisor *lecti sic nutum divitis horret,*
> *sic iterat voces et verba cadentia tollit,*
> *ut puerum saevo credas dictata magistro*
> *reddere vel partes mimum tractare secundas.*

The person here described would occupy one of the two places to the right of the host on the lowest couch (*summus* and *medius in imo*), where he normally placed his dependants. Since the genitive *imi . . . lecti* cannot be objective, we understand 'the mocker on the lowest couch'; cf. *Sat.* II.8.40f. *imi/convivae lecti.* It seems unlikely that a host's parasite would normally have been encouraged or even permitted to make fun of his guests. The wag in *Sat.* 1.4.87f. is regularly brought in evidence, but nothing identifies him as a parasite. Nasidienus' two hangers-on in *Sat.* II.8 do no such thing, though Maecenas' 'shades' (who were not on the lowest couch) covertly mock their host. Here the parasite or client is presented simply as a toady. On the other hand, there is no clear evidence that *derisor* could be used simply for 'parasite'; certainly Plaut. *Capt.* 71 *scio absurde dictum hoc derisores dicere* does not qualify. I wonder therefore whether Horace did not write *divisor.* Sitting next the host, *medius in imo*, the parasite 'divides the lowest couch'. The literal sense of this noun is not found before Apuleius (*De mundo* 1 *axis divisor et disterminator mundi*), but as with *ultor* (see below) the cognate verb legitimises it.

---

[20] Even when client-patron relationship has been established, there are dangers to fear; cf. *Epist.* 1.18.86f. *dulcis inexpertis cultura potentis amici;/expertus metuit.*

Epist. 1.19.39f

non ego nobilium scriptorum auditor et ultor
grammaticas ambire tribus et pulpita dignor

Fraenkel[21] on this 'famous "crux interpretum"' takes *scriptorum* as Horace's Greek models, but his interpretations of
auditor and *ultor* do not convince. If the latter means that
Alcaeus and the rest 'were buried in oblivion until he resusci-
tated their songs in his own odes' (surely not true), how
could they be described as *nobiles*, 'famous'? It is impossible
to understand a reference to future fame, as Fraenkel seems
to do when he compares *Odes* iii.13.13 *fies nobilium tu quoque
fontium* and iv.3.11f. *et spissae nemorum comae/fingent Aeolio
carmine nobilem.* Bentley's interpretation seems to be right:
'et qui vicissim mea recito, sic enim eos ulciscor.' *nobilium* =
notorum (only stronger) does not have to be ironical, but
probably is so to some extent, like *adulescens nobilis* in Cic.
Phil. vi.10 (cf. my *Two Studies in Roman Nomenclature* (1976),
p. 37).

Fraenkel takes no exception to *ultor* = 'requiter, punisher',
which might be difficult to parallel. But it accords with the
common use of *ulcisci*.

Ars 169–73

multa senem circumveniunt incommoda . . .
vel quod res omnes timide gelideque ministrat,   171
dilator, *spe* longus, iners avidusque futuri,
difficilis . . .

Brink obelises *spe longus*: 'Bentley impugned the phrase and
sought to emend it. L. Mueller obelised it. Modern editors
do not; presumably they understand it, though they do not
say how, or if they do they fail.' Attempts at emendation can
be inspected in his note. None seems to me as probable as
spe mancus, 'crippled in hope'. Brink cites Arist. *Rhet.* ii.13,
1390a 4, where old men are said to be δυσέλπιδες διὰ τὴν
ἐμπειρίαν. *Mancus*, a very rare word in poetry, is twice used

[21] Pp. 348f.

by Horace elsewhere. The ablative follows the analogy of *ingenio debilis*.

Ars 319–22

> interdum speciosa locis morataque recte
> fabula nullius veneris, sine *pondere* et arte,   320
> valdius oblectat populum meliusque moratur
> quam versus inopes rerum nugaeque canorae.

Here is a contrast between, on the one hand, a play with well-developed characters and edifying maxims (for the sense of *locis* see Brink) but lacking charm and technical skill —early Roman drama seems to be in mind—and, on the other, 'a melodious trifle, verses without content'. 'Weightlessness' is a characteristic of the latter, not the former. Brink would understand *pondere* as referring to 'weight of diction' (*pondus verborum*) as opposed to 'weight of thought' (*pondus sententiarum*). Nothing in the Latin points to one rather than the other,[22] and any brand of 'weightlessness' ruins the contrast. The text is indefensible.

Metrical weight, due to carelessness or ignorance of 'art' is attributed to Ennius in 258–62:

> hic [spondeus] et in Acci
> nobilibus trimetris apparet rarus et Enni
> in scaenam missos cum magno pondere versus   260
> aut operae celeris nimium curaque carentis
> aut ignoratae premit artis crimine turpi.

In 320 then substitute: *fabula nullius veneris sed pondere inerti*, 'a play of no charm but possessing weight without art'. For the combination of genitive and ablative of quality see Kühner—Stegmann, *Lat. Gramm.* 1.456. *iners = sine arte* ought to be recognised in *Epist.* 1.20.12 *tineas pasces taciturnus inertis*, II.2.126 *scriptor delirus inersque*, and, probably, *A.p.* 445 *versus reprehendet inertis* as well as Prop. II.32.20 *tendis iners docto retia nota mihi* and Ov. *Met.* XIII.694 *inertia vulnera*. The corruption may in fact have started from a gloss *sine arte* on *inertia*.

---

[22] Hence Baxter's note, 'nulla rerum vel verborum gravitate' and Orelli's, 'sine argumenti et generis dicendi gravitate'.

Bentley and Horace[1]

This much can be said for the twentieth century; it is well provided with distinguished anniversaries. And scholars, I suppose, have never been readier to give their time to the praise and appraisal of their predecessors. The fifties bristled with the celebrations of mighty textual critics; and appreciations of their work appear from time to time even without such incidental stimulus—Mr Timpanaro's monograph on the critical method of Lachmann may be mentioned as a recent and outstandingly successful example.

Far from any implication that those who can, do, those who cannot, commemorate, I would willingly eschew the sort of canonisation of the past which, in the sphere of textual criticism, no less than elsewhere, masks injustice to the present. Many scholars, I think, are conscious that progressive elaboration of techniques and the ever increasing quantity of print which must, however unprofitably, be consulted, distracts and hampers them in their congenial employments; but those not engaged on critical work may perhaps need sometimes to be reminded how much the secular accumulation of effort upon a limited number of texts has added to the difficulty and, consequently, the merit of fresh discoveries. *Pereant qui nostra ante nos dixerunt* is a phrase which every generation of classical critics repeats more often and more feelingly. Just over 250 years ago

[1] A lecture in commemoration of Bentley's tercentenary delivered to the Classical Association at Leeds on 11 April 1962 and published in the Proceedings of the Leeds philosophical society (literary and historical section), vol. x, part iii, pp. 105–15; here reprinted with the correction of a misprint, the omission of a Greek citation, and the addition of the footnote on p. 116.

Bentley wrote in the (Latin) preface to his Horace: 'To produce emendations is a far, far harder thing today than it used
to be. Every obvious proposal that suggests itself from a
comparison of manuscripts is already anticipated and fore-
stalled. Scarce anything remains but what must be delved
from the innermost recesses of thought and style, with naught
but wit to aid.' Easy also to forget how often the giants
stumbled. What proportion of Markland's or Madvig's or
the early Housman's conjectures would be printed under an
unknown name in the modern *Classical quarterly*? These men
were often confidently and transparently, though hardly
ever foolishly, wrong. It is of the nature of the critical genius
to function unevenly; and the judgment and self-discipline
to control it are very variously vouchsafed. Bentley is a
notorious case in point. But many scholars lack judgment and
self-discipline without genius to illustrate the deficiency.
Rare and mysterious genius, not ubiquitous defect, claims
emphasis this morning. Perhaps I may be allowed some
general observations on this topic, not I hope altogether
irrelevant to my allotted theme. If there is any better way of
commemorating Bentley than by dwelling, to the best of
one's inadequacy, upon the nature and conditions of that
critical faculty which no other man has possessed in equal
measure, I am not likely to hit upon that way.

I speak of 'genius', not 'Bentley's genius'. In considering a
critic's work, especially on such an occasion as this, one is
tempted to try to fasten upon its individuality. But textual
criticism at its highest is not an art, though there may be an
aesthetic element in its appreciation. 'Corrections such as
these' wrote Bentley's friend Davies of an emendation in the
Eumenides (not, as it happened, a good one), 'are like beautiful
poems.' Now the chasm between creative art and revelatory
science is evident in, among other things, the essential
anonymity of scientific achievement. Scaliger, Bentley,
Porson at their divinatory best shed idiosyncrasy; Leonardo,
Rubens, Chardin did not. Textual critics are individual no
doubt in their shortcomings. You may desiderate fertility in
Porson, elegance in Madvig, *curiosa felicitas* in Lachmann
(though that comes dangerously near to questioning Lach-

mann's title altogether). As for Bentley, 'Had he but the gift
of humility' said his bishop in early days, 'he would be the
most extraordinary man in Europe.' But you cannot say of
any palmary emendation that only one particular critic
could have made it. Even scholars of much inferior calibre,
but still with the divinatory spark inside them—an Arthur
Palmer, an Emil Baehrens, a Friedrich Jacob—could on
their day produce results indistinguishable from those of the
masters, results only by some caprice of chance attainable
by better scholars not so gifted.

I may seem to be tacitly equating criticism with what
Bentley called 'divinandi quaedam peritia et μαντική', what
D. L. Page has called 'the textual critic's greatest gift, that
power of divination which turned δόρυκ' ἀνημέρωι into
δορικανεῖ μόρῳ at Aesch. *Suppl.* 987, κρατεῖς into κάτει at
Medea 1015', what Gilbert Highet rather felicitously called a
glorified form of proof reading. Well, it *is* in divinatory conjecture that the critical faculty shows at its cleanest. It ex-
tends however into cognate activities—into choice between
existing readings and the solution of problems by reinter-
pretation of a sound text. And the critic has tasks which do
not concern the critical faculty at all, some of them, like the
collation of manuscripts, almost mechanical. Others, such
as the arrangement and evaluation of manuscripts, all that
is meant by recension, need other qualities and skills. It is in
this sort of connection that it becomes appropriate to speak of
critical rules and methods, terms which less conservatively
employed make critics reach for their respirators. Not so very
long ago a belief was rife that palaeographical science on one
side and the methods of recension not altogether justly
associated with Lachmann on the other would soon reduce
the editing of classical texts to the application of a set of
established formulae—and how nice that would be for
editors who did not happen to be critics! When Housman
told this Association in 1921 that *criticus nascitur, non fit* and
much else to the same purpose, some of his audience may still
have thought him behind his time. But the limitations of
techniques have become ever more apparent. A livelier
awareness that copyists slip for psychological as well as

scriptorial reasons has checked the spread of paleographical euphoria. At the same time it is less commonly held that recension can normally resolve itself into a neat, reliable arrangement of MSS in a genealogical tree. Pasquali's chapter heading 'recentiores, non deteriores' is one answer to the sneer (I forget whose) at 'Professor Housman, always so ready to find merit in manuscripts and faults in editors'.

Acceptance of these limitations should mean recognition of the paramount role of critical judgment in classical editing. In practice, however, in the general decline of literary scholarship both active and receptive, the contemporary critic is even less assured than his predecessors of an instructed and sympathetic public; while his operations arouse discomfort, as they always did, in non-critical quarters. Moreover the accretion of results and the consequent narrowing of scope for fresh advances has made it almost impossible in the field of classical Latin at least, for learned and industrious non-critics, like say Robinson Ellis, to find corruptions which they can correct. So *divinatio* is still out of fashion, and no one who practices it need expect to be sickened by cheap applause.

What and whence is *divinatio*? Though I used the word 'mysterious' just now, I shall try, conscious of temerity, to attempt some sort of answer. The temperamental basis must be assumed to begin with—no critic will get far without a touch of the critical temper, a questing, malcontent turn, inimical to the gladness of fools and the mendacities of sleeping dogs. But to get further than Zoïlus he needs more. When a fine emendation is conceived, a number of qualities, moral and intellectual, innate and acquired, may cooperate. Housman in 1930 made a list:

Judging an emendation requires in some measure the same qualities as an emendation itself, and the requirement is formidable. To read attentively, think correctly, omit no relevant consideration, and repress self-will, are not ordinary accomplishments; yet an emendator needs much besides: just literary perception, congenial intimacy with the author, experience which must have been won by study, and mother wit which he must have brought from his mother's womb.

Of these attributes I think Housman would have agreed that the heart of the matter is the last. A man might have all the rest in decent measure—had not Jebb?—and yet remain outside the circle. Or he may be glaringly deficient in some—how often did Bentley repress self-will?—and remain the greatest of critics. But mother wit is a rather unspecific term. How elaborate it? Perhaps, at a venture, in some such way as this—

When a novice or a non-critic tries to solve a textual crux, he will generally start with the corruption—juggling with the letters, trying out various palaeographically acceptable substitutions. If the corruption is simple and graphical he may thus stumble on the true reading, though he may very well fail to recognise it as such. The critic on the other hand generally gets his clue from the context. He is faced with a pattern of thought, part of which has been broken up. He has to adjust his mind to that pattern, run it into the mould of the author's as represented in this particular passage. Once that is done, and the correct pattern, so far as it emerges from the context, is established, then, with the help of such indications as the corrupt piece itself provides, and subject to the control of touchstones which knowledge and experience automatically apply, the missing link may suggest itself, often with little conscious effort. The power to run the mind on to a literary context, reacting to and retaining compositely and in due proportion each successive impression —that is as near as I can get to the secret of *divinatio*.

Is this too simple? Contexts are sometimes unrevealing or ambiguous, the pattern may be an elusive, side-lit affair. None the less the critic will nearly always have some idea of the answer he is looking for before he finds it. He begins, as Moriz Haupt said, from the thought—the author's thought re-formed in a sensitive and plastic mind. His apparatus of equipment—learning, taste and so on—is needed at all stages to check results and guard against error. The more efficient it is, the less often he will go wrong; and in some degree it is a prerequisite of contact between author and reader. But it will not do the job. And what is true of removing a recognised corruption is also true of the diagnosis

of corruptions previously unrecognised. The critic as he
reads is all the time adapting his mind to the author's, and
when he feels a jar he suspects that something from outside
has come between.

Well, he has his answer, or thinks he has. That is not the
end. Criticism may be ranked with the revelatory sciences,
but there is the important difference noted by Housman that
when a chemist, say, 'has mixed sulphur and saltpetre and
charcoal in certain proportions and wishes to ascertain if the
mixture is explosive, he need only apply a match', whereas
'our conclusions regarding the truth or falsehood of a reading
can never be confirmed or corrected by an equally decisive
test'. However certain the critic may feel that he is right, he
knows from precedent that his own confidence is no absolute
guarantee. Still less does it guarantee the assent of others,
who will mostly be non-critics. If to judge an emendation
requires something of the same qualities as to make it, small
wonder that some of the best fail of general appreciation.
That is no doubt a hardship to the critic; but then life is hard,
and criticism is rather like life. Probability is the critic's
guide, self-doubt his whispering companion. He may listen,
and stop in his tracks; or he may be deaf, and fall flat on his
face. He is human, and his public even more so. He tries, in
his dusty and sequestered way, to reveal reality by reason;
and reason is often a rush-candle, reality a bugbear. Lives of
great critics all or nearly all remind us that their occupation
can engender certain angularities of temper; perhaps it is
less likely than some other ways of truth-seeking to foster
naïveté in 'human situations'. Perhaps it is a pity that only
one of the breed found time to be a Prime Minister. The
critic in power may turn out selfish, tyrannical, unscrupulous,
but hardly puerile or doctrinaire or muddily conventional.
Better to be a Fellow of Trinity under Bentley than of—but
I am to talk about Bentley's Horace.

He was forty when he undertook the edition, massively
established as the first scholar of the time by his 'Letter to Mill',
his edition of the Callimachean fragments, and his 'Phalaris'.
His critical work had lain almost entirely in Greek. In 1702,
in what many have thought an unlucky hour, he turned to

Latin. 'It is greatly to be regretted,' writes the learned and
judicious Bishop Monk, 'that Bentley should have devoted
so large a proportion of the best years of his life to a Latin,
rather than to a Greek poet: his knowledge and perception
of the latter language was incomparably better than of the
former; and he might have been employed more usefully to
literature, and more honourably to himself, in correcting
real errors in Greek poetry, with a felicity which no one else
could attain, than in suggesting alterations of a Latin author,
and defending them by learning and ingenuity, which
oftener produce admiration than conviction.' With little
claim to pronounce on Bentley as a Hellenist, I permit myself to dissent from this common view. Not that I doubt that,
judged simply by their validity as results, Bentley's Greek
conjectures maintain a more even level. But how far was this
not due to neglect by previous critics of the authors he
favoured? How many of his 5000 conjectures in Hesychius,
made before he was thirty, required a Bentley? It was remarked of a great scholar who was not a great critic that 'he
could restore with ease and felicity a new-found remnant of
Menander, but a much-laboured field like the text of Juvenal
would yield no harvest to his husbandry.' Would Bentley's
peers have venerated him as they always have if he had stuck
to the easier road? Results are not everything, and I do not
think it was a wholly lamentable instinct that led him to
stretch and sometimes overstrain his sinews on Horace,
Terence, Phaedrus, Manilius.

The work went on for four years. Then in 1706 the *text* was
committed to the Cambridge University Press, which, incidentally, has cause to remember Bentley among its greatest
benefactors. The notes appeared after many distractions in
1711, most of them composed within a period of two months
and sent to the printers as they left the author's hand,
'madida fere charta'. He is supposed to have had personal
reasons for haste—to conciliate the public and Lord High
Treasurer Oxford by a resounding literary success at a crisis
in his war with the opposition in Trinity. Such motives were
often suspected in the timing of Bentley's publications:
'whenever he thought himself affronted,' said an enemy, 'he

immediately flung a great book at his adversary.' But in truth his was not the temper of the perfectionist. He knew that fields for his unrivalled powers lay fallow all around him, and no sooner had he torn a swathe through one than he was panting for the next. For the curling tongs, as he said himself, he had neither taste nor time, nor cared much for the starveling credit of a mean meticulosity, 'ieiunam illam obscurae diligentiae laudem.' So his work in general, and certainly his Horace is no exception, bears marks of haste. And the printing of the text prior to the notes committed him to the defence of conjectures which his maturer judgment might have put aside; he did in fact abandon some twenty in his preface. A second and improved edition came out in Amsterdam in 1713.

The notes are concerned with textual points only. But on these Bentley's arsenals of logic and learning were so unsparingly discharged that they spread over a large area of commentary, and what commentary! To praise its acuteness, ingenuity, dialectical force, and illustrative resource would be superfluous. To read those notes, even when they do not extort at least temporary assent, is one of the most stimulating experiences Latin scholarship has to offer. *Mirabilis vir est.* I have read one comparable book, Housman's Manilius, and that was certainly much influenced by Bentley, whom of all successors Housman may be thought to have approached most nearly, however forcefully he himself deprecated comparison. Both wrote Latin with unfailing lucidity (except when read in the climate of Manitoba) and arresting vitality. Compared with Housman's pointed, economical style Bentley's sometimes seems coarse and diffuse. Neither did he set store by classical chastity of diction. He wrote Latin as he did other things, with sovereign ease and large-minded unconcern for inessentials; and his 'mistakes' were reprehended at volume length by contemporary schoolmasters. In his author Bentley will generally be held to have the advantage, even though Manilius deserves Scaliger's praise as 'a most ingenious poet and a most elegant writer', and Housman's mastery of astrological intricacies is caviare to the gourmet. To many readers Bentley's gusto and geniality commend

him; and he repels none by that quasi-emotional dedication
to truth which makes some scholars fidget when Housman's
name is mentioned. Housman does not play practical jokes,
as Bentley does at *Odes* 1.25,11, when he devotes one of his
longest notes to the illustration of a conjecture, only to end
'but let all this be regarded as advanced rather to exercise
the reader's judgment than to maintain that my suggestion
is what Horace actually wrote; for the vulgate, *pace* Scaliger,
can be satisfactorily explained, etc. etc.'.

In round numbers Bentley made 700 changes in the vulgate of his day, of which 500 have some manuscript support,
most of the remainder being conjectures of his own. He
worked when genealogical arrangement of manuscripts was
unthought of, yet in Lachmann's judgment 'everyone who
knows Bentley thoroughly will recognise that a new editor
of Horace, having once eliminated the greater part of
Bentley's own conjectures (no arduous task), will have
scarcely anything further to do, so far as the constitution of
the text is concerned.' That goes rather far. As H. E. Jolliffe
demonstrated in 1939, Bentley sometimes attached more
weight than on his own declared principles he should have
done to the existence of some sort of manuscript authority,
when that authority was in reality negligible. But his judgment of intrinsic merit usually led him aright, and well over
300 of his non-conjectural changes found a permanent place
in the text. The number will surely be higher when Horace is
next edited by a critic. Allowing for the fact that some of
these innovations in the vulgate had been printed by one
previous editor or another, Bentley's textual improvements
alone make his edition a landmark.

Of his conjectures, harsh things are said. Only a very few,
the number varies between 20 and 1, have persuaded his
successors. That, however, reflects on them as well as on him.
Modern Horatian editors, whatever their other merits, have
not been distinguished by critical intelligence. With one
recent and notorious exception they recall Postgate's comparison of Phillimore to 'a furry animal, at repose on a mat
of Berlin wool and gently purring content in front of a fire
which the Marthas of Propertian criticism have made up by

emptying on it again the dust and débris of centuries'. As for the exception, no cat was ever wilder. Looking down Jolliffe's list of universally rejected conjectures by Bentley, I do not despair of the advent of an editor who will not only mention but even follow the proposal at *Odes* II.1.21 (as a matter of fact, it had occurred to Beroaldus two centuries earlier). That is the ode to Pollio, whose *History of the Civil Wars* Horace enthusiastically expects. Already in line 17 Pollio assaults his ears with the threatening clangor of trumpets, already the clarions bray: *iam nunc minaci murmure cornuum/perstringis aures, iam litui strepunt.* Already the horses shy in terror from the sheen of arms and the visages of riders: *iam fulgor armorum fugaces/terret equos equitumque vultus.*

May I digress a moment? I render *vultus* as a nominative, correlative with *fulgor* and subject not object of *terret*, which is unorthodox, though I can hardly suppose it to be original. I do so for two reasons. First Horace would not naturally represent Roman cavalry as terrified by the sheen of arms (I altogether decline to believe that he was thinking of Caesar's instructions at Pharsalia). Second *terret vultus* seems to me implausible as an equivalent of *terret oculos*. *Vultus*, when it means anything besides 'face', connotes expression, especially stern, grim expression (as *Odes* III.3.3 *vultus instantis tyranni*). Expression is hardly to be terrified, but it may terrify, as in *Sat.* II.7.43 *aufer/me vultu terrere*, Cic. *Mil.* 41 *vultu Milonis perterritus*, *Att.* II.8.1 *perterriti voce et vultu*, ibid. XIV.20.5 *non te Bruti nostri vulticulus ab ista oratione deterret?*; cf. also *Odes* I.2.39 *acer et Marsi peditis cruentum/vultus in hostem.*

The vulgate proceeds:

> *audire magnos iam videor duces*
> *non indecoro pulvere sordidos,*
> *et cuncta terrarum subacta*
> *praeter atrocem animum Catonis.*

From the scholiasts on, interpreters have been in two minds about *audire*. Is it 'I seem to hear you, Pollio (or someone else), reading aloud about the generals, etc.'? That ruins Horace's carefully arranged climax. He had not, in imagination, heard anyone read about the bray of the clarions and the terror of the horses; these things were vivid to his senses. And when we come to the generals, the *iam*, a third time reiterated, puts this experience on a par with the others. So a succession of German editors explain that Horace does, in imagination hear the generals—haranguing their troops. They admit that he cannot so well hear the bowing down of all things on earth except Cato's stubborn soul—but after all Cato did *talk* to his friends before committing suicide, or perhaps it is just zeugma. There remains however T. E. Page's point that 'it is as absurd to say "I hear great leaders begrimed etc." as it would be to say "I hear Mr Gladstone in evening dress" '. And I for one should like to know what the generals had been doing to get dusty *before* the speeches. Bentley's way out is simple. Read *videre*. The corruption is quite common, and, as he points out, all this noise of trumpets and clarions was reverberating in the copyist's head—who may also have subconsciously shied away from the unusual short syllable at the start of the line. Bentley adds his usual string of apt parallels for *videre videor*. Here is no master stroke of divinatory genius; but are we to applaud the editors who, with Bentley in front of them, elect to take no notice?

Let me translate the note on III.4.46. Jupiter, says the vulgate Horace, is a god

> *qui terram inertem, qui mare temperat*
> *ventosum et urbes, regnaque tristia;*
> > *divosque mortalesque turbas*
> > *imperio regit unus aequo.*

'Tell me, pray,' says Bentley, 'what *urbes et mortales turbas* is for. Why, it is inept, a mere tautology—unless you were to take *urbes* here, foolishly enough, not as assemblies of human beings but as congeries of wood and stone. Rather read with me and punctuate with an old scholiast

> *qui terram inertem, qui mare temperat*
> *ventosum; et umbras regnaque tristia,*
> > *divosque, mortalesque turbas*
> > *imperio regit unus aequo.'*

There is one ruler for all—gods, men, and the underworld, i.e. *umbras et regna tristia*. Parallels for that expression follow, ending with *Aen.* v.733 *non me impia namque/Tartara habent, tristesque umbrae.*

I should add that Munro sought to justify the vulgate here by citing a fragment of Ennius's *Epicharmus*, which says that Jupiter *mortales atque urbes beluasque omnes iuvat*. But in Ennius progression from men, that is mankind composed of individuals, to cities is perfectly natural, like 'men and tribes and nations' in Housman's funeral hymn. The only value of the comparison is to suggest one possible motive for corruption, if it be assumed that Ennius' line was well known in antiquity. One editor, Kiessling, put *umbras* in his text; but Heinze brought him up to date by restoring *urbes*, with a bare reference to *Odes* II.20.5, where there is no tautology and *urbes* is perfectly apt—better so than Orelli, whose defence of the vulgate text is at loggerheads with his punctuation.

There are conjectures which no editor, not even Bentley himself, has put in his text or ever will, but which only the inconsiderate despise: *auspice Phoebo* for instance in *Odes* I.7.27 *nil desperandum Teucro duce et auspice Teucro*, or *anne Curti* for *an Catonis* at I.12.35. These may be wrong (I should not care to bet a year's pay that they are), but Bentley's scruples remain.

There are other conjectures which certainly *are* wrong, but not therefore unprofitable. In the Cleopatra Ode, I.37 (I continue to take examples from the Odes as most familiar to persons who, like me, are not Horatian specialists), the Queen's courage gets its due at lines 21ff. She did not fear the sword in woman's fashion, nor flee with her swift ships to hidden shores: *nec latentis/classe cita reparavit oras*. What, asks Bentley, as well he may, is *reparavit oras classe*? 'A word,' says Wickham, 'of doubtful sense'; in fact a word of no sense at all. Bentley's *penetravit*, which he contended to be what Horace wrote, 'vel reclamantibus quotquot hodie extant codicibus', is unacceptable, not only palaeographically but because it suggests the daring mariner rather than the fugitive queen. But if we cannot take *properavit* or think of anything better, let us put up our daggers with acknowledgments to Bentley.[2]

At line 9 of the same Ode, *contaminato cum grege turpium/ morbo virorum*, Bentley's interpretation of *morbo* as unnatural vice is generally admitted; his contention that Cleopatra's eunuchs would not be called *viri* is in my judgment no less clearly valid, and when he says 'in illa locutione, *virorum turpium morbo*, non agnosco elegantiam Flacci' I applaud his taste, yes, Bentley's taste, of which more presently. Nobody however is going to substitute his *opprobriorum* for *morbo virorum*; but someone may yet be led by Bentley to a better answer. I have sometimes wondered whether a comma after *turpium* may not be that answer: 'her crew of foul creatures, men only in vice, *morbo virorum*). Augustus's companions were warriors, *viri*; Cleopatra's were *semiviri*, warriors in one thing, *morbo*, and in that one thing only. *hic*, says Propertius, meaning 'in bed', *hic ego Pelides, hic ferus Hector ego.*

Bentley was one of the most learned men who ever lived, but sometimes his knowledge was too little, and so dangerous, as in his long note on *Odes* 1.3.18 about the dauntless sailor who sees the monsters of the deep without a tear, *siccis oculis*. Greek and Latin literature is plundered to prove that *siccis* ought to be, must be, *rectis*. It is very persuasive (it persuaded Porson), unless one remembers or finds out from Orelli that the ancients *did* think it natural to weep at the immediate prospect of death, witness Propertius, Ovid, Curtius, Euripides. Bentley's suspicions were misplaced, but Horatian commentaries are the gainers.

The associated charges of pedantic cavilling and lack of poetic taste have stuck to Bentley's Horace, not, of course, altogether undeservedly. The burlesque of his style and practice in Richard Johnson's 'Aristarchus Anti-Bentleianus' is so amusing that I take a passage from Monk's note *en bloc*:

---

[2] In their edition of *Odes* I (1970) Nisbet—Hubbard defend *reparavit* as ' "took in exchange", and hence "reached" ' by the analogous uses of Greek ἀμείβειν and ἀλλάσσειν and a Latin verse inscription in Buecheler's *Carmina epigraphica* (258). Agreed, though the sense assumed in the inscription is hardly certain, and was in fact firmly rejected by Buecheler.

And now my hand's in, after the example of great authors, and the Doctor in particular, I shall not think much of my labour, for the reader's benefit, the honour of the English nation in general and the family of the Bostocks in particular, to put down one stanza of a certain English Marine Ode, for so in good truth it is, and so it is entituled in all the parchments, and the first editions; how in the latter it came to be called a Ballad, I for my part can't tell; let them look to it that were the cause of it. But 'tis high time to put down the place. Why so it runs then,

> Then old Tom Bostock he fell to the work,
> He prayed like a Christian, but fought like a Turk,
> And cut 'em off all in a jerk,
> > Which nobody can deny, etc.

Now you must understand, this Tom Bostock was chaplain, in Latin *capellanus*, in a sea-fight, a long time ago, and after the enemy had boarded the ship, cut 'em all off to a man. O bravo Tom! Thus much for the interpretation. Now to the reading.

Old. I have a shrewd suspicion that all is not sound at bottom here; how sound a complexion soever the words may seem to have. For why *old*, pray ye? What, he hewed down so many lusty fellows at fourscore, I'll warrant ye?

A likely story. I know there is *old boy*, as well as any of ye: but what then? And I could down with *old Tom* in another place, but not here.

For once again, I say, why *old* Tom? What, when he was commending him for so bold an action, would he rather say, *old* Tom, than *bold* Tom? Was it not a bold action? Is not the word *bold* necessary in this place? And do you find it anywhere else? Thou, therefore, ne'er be afraid of being too bold, no, rather boldly read *bold* Tom, I'll bear thee out; in Latin, *me vide.* But you'll say, neither edition, nor manuscript hath this reading; I thought as much.

What of all that? I suppose we have never a copy under the author's own hand: as for the librarians and editors, what can you expect from such cattle as they but such stuff as this? One grain of sense (and God be thanked I don't want that) weighs more with me than a tun of their papers.

A good joke, but no more. For one thing Bentley was not dealing with the *Ballad of Tom Bostock.* The tools that mend a watch are not designed for quarrying slate. Bentley's operations on the text of Horace were not frivolous; his case for a change can sometimes be refuted, hardly ever dismissed as unworthy of refutation. His poetic taste, or rather lack of it, is a byword. Even so wholehearted an admirer as Housman used freely to confess the deficiency, and could call him, not wholly in irony, 'this tasteless pedant'—Housman, who was ready for chop-logic's sake to spoil Propertius's most haunting hexameter. Here, I suggest, is a matter for careful distinction. Let us leave Milton out of it. Bentley's taste was formed by Greek and Latin; small wonder that he came to grief when he had the temerity to meddle with so radically unclassical a poet. What about Horace? If you read a Latin poet as edited by Baehrens, or, extremes meeting, by one of those Buecheleriastri to whom Baehrens was anathema, you will constantly be meeting grotesqueries which take your eyes to the bottom of the page, there usually to find that they belong to the editor or the copyist respectively. If Horace existed only in Bentley's text I suspect that critical readers would very seldom be so discomposed. A thing like *duro numine* in *Odes* III.10.8 is quite exceptional. Bentley had, I believe, as good a nose as any for the kind of thing which most Latin poets, Ovid for example, would or would not write. But for Horace this was not enough. When I hear people read from Emily Brontë about joy growing mad with awe in counting future tears, I *should* be prepared to bet a year's pay that the word intended was 'sad', not 'mad'; and if I am shown 'mad' in her microscopic autograph, I shall remain obdurate, and talk of *lapsus calami*. For Emily Brontë was a great poet in virtue of other gifts than that of the magical word, let alone the sophisticated and designedly puzzling word. In her case I should hold it perverse to cast about for a latent meaning or beauty in the superficially nonsensical 'mad'. But there have been poets, Virgil say and Shakespeare, who used the word that others would not have thought of with an incalculable success that reaches the heart of poetry. And there are poets, how many there are, who have to avoid the ordinary expression because it is ordinary. Horace perhaps has a seat at both these tables. His *felicitas* was *curiosa*. For this characteristic Bentley had insufficient appreciation. *amara leni/temperet risu* at *Odes* II.16.26 is an unexceptionable phrase; but Horace was not always content with the unexceptionable, and chose to write *lento risu*.

When all is said, and how little I have been able to say, this great book vindicates itself; not only by the amount of Latin it still can teach—I forget who said that he learned more from Bentley wrong than from anyone else right—but by the quality of the intellectual experience it offers the reader. The writer too had his experience. If Bentley were alive now he might not be a classical scholar. In his own time this many-sided colossus proved his potentialities as theologian, mathematician, lawyer. But if he *were* a classical scholar, I believe he would still be a critic, *animi causa*. He would not be deterred by being told that our texts are 'good enough to live with'. Maybe they are, maybe they were three hundred years ago. So much depends on one's standard of living. But they can be made better, and, where sound, better explained; let it never be forgotten that emendation and interpretation are Siamese twins. This end, followed with vigilance, intelligence, tact, and responsibility, keeps alive (as what else will?) a just and familiar understanding of the two languages and literatures, that penetration of the 'intima sententiae vis et orationis indoles' from which Bentley said that good conjectures must be delved. But results, direct or indirect, are not everything, certainly not to classical scholars, whose most altruistic endeavours will never enlarge a bomb or a television screen. *The Times* may ask whether we shall appreciate Ovid any the more when Mr Kenney has arranged his manuscripts. I dare say we shan't, but then Ovid, unless he was a very unusual poet, did not make his verses philanthropically, but because he liked making them and knew the trick. He might indeed have grown discouraged if nobody had taken any interest, but that was not his case, neither is it Mr Kenney's. And what is to happen when the last manuscript is placed or unplaceable, the last crux solved or despaired? I do not know, any more than I know what will happen when the last tenth of a second is pared off the mile record, *neque aeternis minorem/consiliis animum fatigo*. Meanwhile, and it will be long enough, there is room for Bentleys. A subject does not survive on appreciation. The cause of the classics is not to be saved or served by ignoring Postgate's valedictory reminder 'that truth is the most powerful solvent, and its pursuit the most potent motive that the world has known; that studies decay the moment that they cease to grow; and that there is a doom awaiting the intellectual as surely as the moral Sybaris.'

Latin texts of passages quoted only in translation

p. 2   *Epist.* i.19.23–5

Parios ego primus iambos
ostendi Latio, numeros animosque secutus
Archilochi, non res et agentia verba Lycamben.

p. 4   *Epod.* 12.21–4

muricibus Tyriis iteratae vellera lanae
cui properabantur? tibi nempe,
ne foret aequalis inter conviva, magis quem
diligeret mulier sua quam te.

p. 6   *Epod.* 3.19–22

at si quid umquam tale concupiveris,
iocose Maecenas, precor,
manum puella savio opponat tuo,
extrema et in sponda cubet.

p. 10   *Sat.* ii.1.30–4

ille velut fidis arcana sodalibus olim
credebat libris, neque, si male cesserat, usquam
decurrens alio, neque si bene ; quo fit ut omnis
votiva pateat veluti descripta tabella
vita senis.

p. 12   Ps.-Acro on *Sat.* i.2.31

Catone transeunte quidam exiit de fornice ; quem, cum
fugit, revocavit et laudavit. postea cum frequentius eum

exeuntem de eodem lupanari vidisset, dixit: 'adulescens,
*ego te laudavi tamquam hic intervenires, non tamquam hic
habitares.*

pp. 15f.   *Sat.* 1.6.52–62

> *felicem dicere non hoc
> me possim, casu quod te sortitus amicum;
> nulla etenim mihi te fors obtulit. optimus olim
> Vergilius, post hunc Varius dixere quid essem.
> ut veni coram, singultim pauca locutus
> (infans namque pudor prohibebat plura profari),
> non ego me claro natum patre, non ego circum
> me Satureiano vectari rura caballo,
> sed quod eram narro; respondes, ut tuus est mos,
> pauca; abeo, et revocas nono post mense iubesque
> esse in amicorum numero.*

p. 18   Cic. *Ad fam.* III.7.5

*superiorem quidem numquam, sed parem vobis me speravi
esse factum. . . . tu si aliter existimas, nihil errabis si
paulo diligentius, ut quid sit* εὐγένεια *[quid sit nobilitas]
intellegas, Athenodorus, Sandonis filius, quid de his rebus
dicat attenderis.*

p. 18   *Sat.* 1.6.19–21

> *namque esto, populus Laevino mallet honorem
> quam Decio mandare novo, censorque moveret
> Appius, ingenuo si non essem patre natus.*

p. 18   *Sat.* 1.6.22

vel merito, quoniam in propria non pelle quiessem.

pp. 18f.   *Sat.* 1.6.45–8

> *nunc ad me redeo libertino patre natum,
> quem rodunt omnes libertino patre natum,
> nunc quia sum tibi, Maecenas, convictor, at olim
> quod mihi pareret legio Romano tribuno.*

p. 19   *Sat.* 1.6.62–4

> magnum hoc ego duco
> quod placui tibi, qui turpi secernis honestum,
> non patre praeclaro, sed vita et pectore puro.

p. 19   *Sat.* 1.6.89

nil me paeniteat sanum patris huius

pp. 19f. *Sat.* 1.6.112–31

incedo solus, percontor quanti holus ac far.
fallacem circum vespertinumque pererro
saepe forum, adsisto divinis. inde domum me
ad porri et ciceris refero laganique catinum.
cena ministratur pueris tribus et lapis albus
pocula cum cyatho duo sustinet, adstat echinus
vilis, cum patera guttus, Campana supellex.
deinde eo dormitum, non sollicitus mihi quod cras
surgendum sit mane . . .
ad quartam iaceo; post hanc vagor, aut ego lecto
aut scripto quod me tacitum iuvet unguor olivo,
non quo fraudatis immundus Natta lucernis.
ast ubi me fessum sol acrior ire lavatum
admonuit, fugio Campum lusumque trigonem.
pransus non avide, quantum interpellet inani
ventre diem durare, domesticus otior. haec est
vita solutorum misera ambitione gravique;
his me consolor victurum suavius ac si
quaestor avus pater atque meus patruusque fuisset.

p. 21   *Sat.* 1.9.22–5

si bene me novi, non Viscum pluris amicum,
non Varium facies. nam quis me scribere pluris
aut citius possit versus? quis membra movere
mollius? invideat quod et Hermogenes ego canto.

p. 21   *Sat.* 1.4.34

faenum habet in cornu, longe fuge!

p. 21   *Sat.* 1.9.43–8

'*Maecenas quomodo tecum?*'
hinc repetit; 'paucorum hominum et mentis bene sanae;
nemo dexterius fortuna est usus. haberes
magnum adiutorem, posset qui ferre secundas,
hunc hominem velles si tradere. dispeream ni
submosses omnis.'

p. 22   *Sat.* 1.9.48–53

non isto vivimus illic
quo tu rere modo. domus hac nec purior ulla est
nec magis his aliena malis. nil mi officit, inquam,
ditior hic aut est quia doctior; est locus uni
cuique suus.' '*magnum narras, vix credibile.*' '*atqui*
sic habet.'

p. 23   *Sat.* 1.3.19f.

nunc aliquis dicat mihi: 'quid tu?
nullane habes vitia?' *immo alia, et fortasse—minora.*

p. 25   *Sat.* 1.1.24f.

quamquam ridentem dicere verum
quid vetat?

p. 27   *Sat.* 1.1.80–3

at si condoluit temptatum frigore corpus
aut alius casus lecto te affixit, habes qui
adsideat, fomenta paret, medicum roget, ut te
suscitet ac reddat natis carisque propinquis.

p. 27   *Epist.* 1.1.76–83

belua multorum es capitum. nam quid sequar aut quem?
pars hominum gestit conducere publica, sunt qui
frustis et pomis viduas venentur avaras
excipiantque senes, quos in vivaria mittant,
multis occulto crescit res faenore. verum
esto aliis alios rebus studiisque teneri:
idem eadem possunt horam durare probantes?

p. 28   *Od.* III.16.21–4

quanto quisque sibi plura negaverit,
ab dis plura feret: nil cupientium
nudus castra peto et transfuga divitum
partes linquere gestio

p. 28   *Od.* III.16.37f.

importuna tamen pauperies abest,
nec, si plura velim, tu dare deneges.

p. 30   *Sat.* I.10.17–19

quos neque pulcher
Hermogenes umquam legit, neque simius iste
nil praeter Calvum et doctus cantare Catullum.

p. 30   *Sat.* I.10. *1–4

Lucili, quam sis mendosus, teste Catone,
defensore tuo, pervincam, qui male factos
emendare parat versus

pp. 32f.   *Sat.* II.1.39–46

sed hic stilus haud petet ultro
quemquam animantem et me veluti custodiet ensis
vagina tectus; quem cur destringere coner
tutus ab infestis latronibus? o pater et rex
Iuppiter, ut pereat positum robigine telum,
nec quisquam noceat cupido mihi pacis! at ille
qui me commorit (melius non tangere, clamo),
flebit et insignis tota cantabitur urbe.

p. 33   *Sat.* II.1.57–60

ne longum faciam: seu me tranquilla senectus
exspectat seu Mors atris circumvolat alis,
dives inops, Romae seu fors ita iusserit exul,
quisquis erit vitae scribam color.

p. 34   *Sat.* II.1.12–15

       cupidum, pater optime, vires
deficiunt. neque enim quivis horrentia pilis
agmina nec fracta pereuntis cuspide Gallos
aut labentis equo describit vulnera Parthi.

p. 34   *Sat.* II.1.17–20

       haud mihi deero,
cum res ipsa feret. nisi dextro tempore Flacci
verba per attentam non ibunt Caesaris aurem,
cui male si palpere, recalcitrat undique tutus.

p. 37   *Sat.* II.6.14f.

pingue pecus domino facias et cetera praeter
ingenium.

p. 37   *Sat.* II.6.28–62

luctandum in turba et facienda iniuria tardis.
quid tibi vis, insane, et quas res improbus urges
iratis pedibus? tu pulses omne quod obstat,
ad Maecenatem memori si mente recurras?
hoc iuvat et melli est, non mentiar. at simul atras
ventum est Esquilias, aliena negotia centum
per caput et circa saliunt latus. 'ante secundam
Roscius orabat sibi adesses ad Puteal cras.'
'de re communi scribae magna atque nova te
orabant hodie meminisses, Quinte, reverti.'
'imprimat his cura Maecenas signa libellis.'
dixeris 'experiar', 'si vis, potes' addit et instat.
   Septimus octavo propior iam fugerit annus
ex quo Maecenas me coepit habere suorum
in numero, dumtaxat ad hoc, quem tollere raeda
vellet iter faciens et cui concredere nugas
hoc genus: 'hora quota est?', 'Thraex est Gallina Syro par?',
matutina parum cautos iam frigora mordent',
et quae rimosa bene deponuntur in aure.
per totum hoc tempus subiectior in diem et horam
invidiae noster. ludos spectaverat una,
luserat in Campo, 'Fortunae filius' omnes.

frigidus a rostris manat per compita rumor :
quicumque obvius est, me consulit : 'o bone (nam te
scire, deos quoniam propius contingis, oportet),
numquid de Dacis audisti ?' 'nil equidem.' 'ut tu
semper eris derisor !' 'at omnes di exagitent me,
si quicquam !' 'quid ? militibus promissa Triquetra
praedia Caesar an est Itala tellure daturus ?'
iurantem me scire nihil mirantur ut unum
scilicet egregii mortalem altique silenti.
perditur haec inter misero lux, non sine votis :
'o rus, quando ego te aspiciam quandoque licebit
nunc veterum libris, nunc somno et inertibus horis
ducere sollicitae iucunda oblivia vitae ?'

p. 39   *Sat.* II.3.13

invidiam placare paras virtute relicta ?

p. 39   *Sat.* II.3.321–6

adde poemata nunc, hoc est, oleum adde camino,
quae si quis sanus fecit, sanus facis et tu.
non dico horrendam rabiem. 'iam desine !' cultum
maiorem censu. 'teneas, Damasippe tuis te.'
mille puellarum, puerorum mille furores.
'o maior, tandem parcas, insane, minori !'

p. 40   Cic. *Ad Att.* I.17.2

nam quanta sit in Quinto, fratre meo, comitas, quanta
iucunditas, quam mollis animus et ad accipiendam et ad
deponendam offensionem, nihil attinet me ad te, qui ea
nosti, scibere.

p. 40   Cic. *Ad Att.* I.17.4

nam si ita statueris, et irritabilis animos esse optimorum
saepe hominum et eosdem placabilis, et esse hanc agilitatem,
ut ita dicam, mollitiamque naturae plerumque bonitatis . . .
facile haec, quemadmodum spero, mitigabuntur.

p. 41   *Sat.* ii.7.72–4

'non sum moechus' ais: neque ego hercule fur, ubi vasa
praetereo sapiens argentea. tolle periclum,
iam vaga prosiliet frenis natura remotis.

p. 41   *Sat.* ii.7.89–94

quinque talenta
poscit te mulier, vexat, foribusque repulsum
perfundit gelida, rursus vocat. eripe turpi
colla iugo. 'liber, liber sum' dic age! non quis.
urget enim dominus mentem non lenis et acris
subiectat lasso stimulos versatque negantem.

p. 43   *Sat.* ii.7.111–18

adde quod idem
non horam tecum esse potes, non otia recte
ponere, teque ipsum vitas fugitivus et erro,
iam vino quaerens, iam somno fallere curam.
frustra; nam comes atra premit sequiturque fugacem.
'unde mihi lapidem?' quorsum est opus? 'unde sagittas?'
aut insanit homo aut versus facit. 'ocius hinc te
ni rapis, accedes opera agro nona Sabino'.

p. 46   *Od.* i.22.13–16

quale portentum neque militaris
Daunias latis alit aesculetis,
nec Iubae tellus generat, leonum
arida nutrix.

p. 47   *Od.* ii.13.1–12

ille et nefasto te posuit die,
quicumque primum et sacrilega manu
produxit, arbos, in nepotum
perniciem opprobriumque pagi,

illum et parentis crediderim sui
fregisse cervicem et penetralia
sparsisse nocturno cruore
hospitis; ille venena Colcha

et quidquid usquam concipitur nefas
tractavit, agro qui statuit meo
te, triste lignum, te caducum
in domini vaput immerentis.

p. 48   *Od.* 1.34.5–12

namque Diespiter
igni corusco nubila dividens
plerumque, per purum tonantis
egit equos volucremque currum,

quo bruta tellus et vaga flumina,
quo Styx et invisi horrida Taenari
sedes Atlanteusque finis
concutitur.

p. 48   *Od.* II.19.1–4

Bacchum in remotis carmina rupibus
vidi docentem, credite posteri,
nymphasque discentis et auris
capripedum satyrorum acutas.

p. 49   *Epist.* 1.19.9–11

'*adimam cantare severis.*'
hoc simul edixi, non cessavere poetae
nocturno cantare mero, putere diurno.

p. 49   *Epist.* 1.19.19f.

o imitatores, servum pecus! ut mihi saepe
bilem, saepe iocum vestri movere tumultus!

p. 49   *Epist.* 1.19.35f.

scire velis, mea cur ingratus opuscula lector
laudet ametque domi, premat extra limen iniquus?

p. 50   *Epist.* 1.19.41–9

'*spissis indigna theatris*
scripta pudet recitare et nugis addere pondus'
*si dixi, '*rides*' ait '*et Iovis auribus ista*

servas. fidis enim manare poetica mella
te solum, tibi pulcher.' ad haec ego naribus uti
formido et, luctantis acuto ne secer ungui,
'displicet iste locus' clamo et diludia posco.
ludus enim genuit trepidum certamen et iram,
ira truces inimicitias et funebre bellum.

p. 50   *Sat.* 1.10.76f.

non ego. nam satis est equitem mihi plaudere, ut audax
contemptis aliis explosa Arbuscula dixit.

p. 53   *Epist.* 1.7.1–2

quinque dies tibi pollicitus me rure futurum,
Sextilem totum mendax desideror.

p. 53   *Epist.* 1.7.10–13

quod si bruma nives Albanis illinet agris,
ad mare descendet vates tuus et sibi parcet
contractusque leget; te, dulcis amice, reviset
cum Zephyris, si concedes, et hirundine prima.

p. 53   *Epist.* 1.7.14–24

non quo more piris vesci Calaber iubet hospes
tu me fecisti locupletem. 'vescere, sodes.'
'iam satis est.' 'at tu quantum vis tolle.'
                              'benigne.'
'non invisa feres pueris munuscula parvis.'
'tam teneor dono quam si dimittar onustus.'
'ut libet; haec porcis hodie comedenda relinques.'
prodigus et stultus donat quae spernit et odit:
haec seges ingratos tulit et feret omnibus annis.
vir bonus et sapiens dignis ait esse paratus
nec tamen ignorat quid distent aera lupinis.
dignum praestabo me etiam pro laude merentis.

p. 54   *Epist.* 1.7.35f.

nec somnum plebis laudo satur altilium nec
otia divitiis Arabum liberrima muto.

p. 55   *Epist.* 1.7.37–9

saepe verecundum laudasti rexque paterque
audisti coram nec verbo parcius absens :
inspice si possum donata reponere laetus.

pp. 57f.   *Epist.* 1.7.44f.

parvum parva decent. mihi iam non regia Roma
sed vacuum Tibur placet aut imbelle Tarentum.

p. 58   *Epist.* 1.7.96–8

qui semel aspexit quantum dimissa petitis
praestent, mature redeat repetatque relicta.
metiri se quemque suo modulo ac pede verum est.

p. 60   *Epist.* 1.18.106–12

quid sentire putas, quid credis, amice, precari?
sit mihi quod nunc est, etiam minus, ut mihi vivam
quod superest aevi, si quid superesse volunt di ;
sit bona librorum et provisae frugis in annum
copia neu fluitem dubiae spe pendulus horae.
sed satis est orare Iovem quae ponit et aufert.
det vitam, det opes : aequum mi animum ipse parabo.

p. 61   *Epist.* 1.14.4f.

certemus spinas animone ego fortius an tu
evellas agro, et melior sit Horatius an res.

p. 61   *Sat.* 11.7.28f.

Romae rus optas, absentem rusticus urbem
tollis ad astra levis.

p. 61   *Epist.* 1.8.12

Romae Tibur amem, ventosus Tibure Roman.

p. 62 *Epist.* II.2.65–76

praeter cetera, me Romaene poemata censes
scribere posse inter tot curas totque labores?
hic sponsum vocat, hic auditum scripta relictis
omnibus officiis. cubat hic in colle Quirini,
hic extremo in Aventino, visendus uterque;
intervalla vides humane commoda. verum
purae sunt plateae, nihil ut meditantibus obstet:
festinat calidus mulis gerulisque redemptor,
torquet nunc lapidem, nunc ingens machina tignum,
tristia robustis luctantur funera plaustris,
hac rabiosa fugit canis, hac lutulenta ruit sus.
i nunc et versus tecum meditare canoros!

p. 62. *Epist.* I.14.40–5

cum servis urbana diaria rodere mavis,
horum tu in numerum voto ruis; invidet usum
lignorum et pecoris tibi calo argutus et horti.
optat ephippia bos piger, optat arare caballus.
quam scit uterque, libens censebo exerceat artem.

p. 62 *Epist.* I.6.15f.

insani sapiens nomen ferat, aequus iniqui,
ultra quam satis est virtutem si petat ipsam.

pp. 62f. *Epist.* I.6.28–32

si latus aut renes morbo temptantur acuto,
quaere fugam morbi! vis recte vivere. quis non?
si virtus hoc una potest dare, fortis omissis
hoc age deliciis. virtutem verba putas et
lucum ligna: cave ne portus occupet alter.

p. 63 *Epist.* I.6.56–62

si bene qui cenat bene vivit, lucet, eamus
quo ducit gula . . .
                    . . . crudi tumidique lavemur,
quid deceat, quid non obliti

p. 63   *Epist.* 1.8.3f.

si quaeret quid agam, dic multa et pulchra minantem
vivere nec recte nec suaviter

p. 63   *Epist.* 1.10.44–6

laetus sorte tua vives sapienter, Aristi,
nec me dimittes incastigatum, ubi plura
cogere quam satis est ac non cessare videbor.

p. 64   *Epist.* 1.15.42–6

nam tuta et parvula laudo,
cum res deficiunt, satis inter vilia fortis.
verum ubi quid melius contingit et unctius, idem
vos sapere et solos aio bene vivere, quorum
conspicitur nitidis fundata pecunia villis.

p. 64   *Epist.* 1.4.16

Epicuri de grege porcum.

p. 64   *Epist.* 1.15.17–21

rure meo possum quidvis perferre patique :
ad mare cum veni, generosum et lene requiro,
quod curas abigat, quod cum spe divite manet
in venas animumque meum, quod verba ministret,
quod me Lucanae iuvenem commendet amicae.

p. 64   *Epist.* 1.20.20–5

me libertino natum patre et in tenui re
maiores pinnas nido extendisse loqueris,
ut, quantum generi demas, virtutibus addas;
me primis Urbis belli placuisse domique,
corporis exigui, praecanum, solibus aptum,
irasci celerem, tamen ut placabilis essem.

p. 64   *Sat.* II.1.75–7

> *tamen me*
> *cum magnis vixisse invita fatebitur usque*
> *Invidia*

p. 64   *Epist.* I.17.35

principibus placuisse viris non ultima laus est.

pp. 64f.   *Vita Horatii*

sume tibi aliquid iuris apud me, tamquam si convictor mihi fueris. recte enim et non temere feceris, quoniam id usus mihi tecum esse volui, si per valetudinem tuam fieri possit.

p. 65   *Vita Horatii*

tui qualem habeam memoriam, poteris ex Septimio quoque nostro audire. nam incidit ut illo coram fieret a me tui mentio. neque enim si tu superbus amicitiam nostram sprevisti, ideo nos quoque ἀνθυπερηφανοῦμεν

pp. 65f.   *Epist.* I.11.7–10

> *scis Lebedus quid sit? Gabiis desertior atque*
> *Fidenis vicus: tamen illic vivere vellem*
> *oblitusque meorum, obliviscendus et illis,*
> *Neptunum procul e terra spectare furentem.*

p. 67   *Od.* IV.1.33–40

> *sed cur, heu Ligurine, cur*
> *manat rara meas lacrima per genas?*
> *cur facunda parum decoro*
> *inter verba cadit lingua silentio?*
> *nocturnis ego somniis*
> *iam captum teneo, iam volucrem sequor*
> *te per gramina Martii*
> *Campi, te per aquas, dure, volubilis.*

p. 69   Cic. *Tusc.* IV.70f.

*sed poetas ludere sinamus, quorum fabulis in hoc flagitio
versari ipsum videmus Iovem. ad magistros virtutis philoso-
phos veniamus, qui amorem negant stupri esse et in eo
litigant cum Epicuro non multum, ut opinio mea fert,
mentiente. quis est enim iste amor amicitiae? cur neque
deformem adulescentem quisquam amat neque formosum
senem? mihi quidem haec in Graecorum gymnasiis nata
consuetudo videtur, in quibus isti liberi et concessi sunt amores (bene ergo Ennius 'flagiti principium est nudare inter
civis corpora'). qui ut sint, quod fieri posse video, pudici,
solliciti tamen et anxii sunt, eoque magis quod se ipsi
continent et coercent. atque ut muliebris amores omittam,
quibus maiorem licentiam natura concessit, quis aut de
Ganymedi raptu dubitat quid poetae velint aut non intellegit
quid apud Euripidem et loquatur et cupiat Laius? quid
denique homines doctissimi et summi poetae de se ipsis et
carminibus edunt et cantibus? fortis vir in sua re publica
cognitus quae de iuvenum amore scribit Alcaeus! nam Ana-
creontis quidem tota poesis est amatoria. maxime vero
omnium flagrasse amore Reginum Ibycum apparet ex scriptis.*

p. 70   Cic. *Off.* 1.144

*bene Pericles, cum haberet collegam in praetura Sophoclem
eique de communi officio convenissent et casu formosus puer
praeteriret dixissetque Sophocles 'o puerum pulchrum,
Pericle!', 'at enim praetorem, Sophocle, decet non solum
manus sed etiam oculos abstinentis habere.' atque hoc idem
Sophocles si in athletarum probatione dixisset, iusta
reprehensione caruisset. tanta vis est et loci et temporis.*

pp. 70f. Cic. *Nat. d.* 1.79

*quotus enim quisque formosus est? Athenis cum essem, e
gregibus epheborum vix singuli reperiebantur. video quid
arriseris, sed ita tamen se res habet. deinde nobis qui con-
cedentibus philosophis antiquis adulescentulis delectamur
etiam vitia saepe iucunda sunt. . . . Q. Catulus, huius
collegae et familiaris nostri pater, dilexit municipem tuum
Roscium, in quem etiam illud est eius . . . huic deo pulchrior; at erat, sicuti hodie est, perversissimis oculis. quid
refert, si hoc ipsum salsum illi et venustum videbatur?*

pp. 71f.   Plin. *Epist.* vii.4.6

Cum libros Galli legerem, quibus ille parenti
ausus de Cicerone dare est palmamque decusque,
lascivum inveni lusum Ciceronis et illo
spectandum ingenio, quo seria condidit et quo
humanis salibus multo varioque lepore
magnorum ostendit mentes gaudere virorum.
nam queritur, quod fraude mala frustratus amantem
paucula cenato sibi debita savia Tiro
tempore nocturno subtraxerit. his ego lectis
'cur post haec' inquam 'nostros celamus amores
nullumque in medium timidi damus atque fatemur
Tironisque dolos, Tironis nosse fugaces
blanditias et furta novas addentia flammas?'

p. 75   Quint. *Inst.* x. 1.100

utinam non inquinasset argumenta puerorum foedis amoribus
mores suos fassus.

p. 78   *Epist.* ii.2.41–57

Romae nutriri mihi contigit atque doceri
iratus Graiis quantum nocuisset Achilles.
adiecere bonae paulo plus artis Athenae,
scilicet ut vellem curvo dinoscere rectum
atque inter silvas Academi quaerere verum.
dura sed emovere loco me tempora grato,
civilisque rudem belli tulit aestus in arma
Caesaris Augusti non responsura lacertis.
unde simul primum me dimisere Philippi,
decisis humilem pennis inopemque paterni
et laris et fundi paupertas impulit audax
ut versus facerem. sed quod non desit habentem
quae poterunt umquam satis expurgare cicutae,
ni melius dormire putem quam scribere versus?

Addendum

Odes IV.5.17–20 (*Divis orte bonis*)

> *tutus bos etenim rura perambulat,*
> *nutrit rura Ceres almaque Faustitas,*
> *pacatum volitant per mare navitae,*
> *culpari metuit Fides*

Housman remarks in a well-known passage of the introduction to his edition of Lucan (p. xxxiii): 'Horace was as sensitive to iteration as any modern; and those who choose to believe that he wrote *tutus bos etenim rura perambulat, nutrit rura Ceres*, which not even Lucan could have written, are as blind to truth as to beauty.' In his review (*Gnomon* 2 (1926).507) Fraenkel took this for a covert recommendation of Bentley's *farra* in 18, which it is not. Housman could not away with *rura . . . rura*, but his unwillingness to mention any conjecture (there are several) suggests that none of them was altogether to his liking.

The repetition could only be deliberate; but what could Horace be about? 'Tecum cogita, ecquam gratiam et venerem habeat ista repetitio. Mihi quidem *rura rura* rus merum et librariorum stuporem sapere videtur' (Bentley). The common defence (Orelli etc.) is, in effect, that the repetition of the word marks Horace's concern with agriculture. But even someone interested in whisky is hardly likely to say: 'John drinks whisky all day, Henry prefers whisky to rum.' But anyone might say: 'John drinks whisky all day, Henry won't have whisky in the house.' *rura . . . rura* can be maintained only by showing a *significant* link between the behaviour of the ox (or cow) and the behaviour of Ceres, as by way of contrast.

The link exists. As the ox roves, it grazes; it takes nourishment from the land. Ceres, by contrast, puts nourishment
(seed) into the land. Both in their opposite ways contribute to
rural welfare. The point would be easier for a Roman reader
to pick up because of the special association, amounting
almost to equivalence, between roving and grazing (*errare*
and *pasci*) in pastoral verse. On that I need only refer to
R. F. Thomas' ingenious and instructive paper 'Theocritus,
Calvus, and *Eclogue* 6' in *Cl. Phil.* 74 (1979). 337f.

Indexes

1. General[1]

adiaphoria, 35
Afranius, 75
Albius (Tibullus?), 65
Alcaeus, 44, 47, 69
Alfius, 5
Anacreon, 44, 69
Anderson, W. S., 15
Appius Claudius, 17f.
Arbuscula, 50
Archilochus, 2–7, 10
Aristippus, 60
Aristius Fuscus, 65
Aristophanes, 6, 27
Aristotle, 40, 48
Asinius Gallus, 71f., 74
Asinius Pollio, 71
Augustus, *see* Caesar Augustus

Baehrens, E., 106, 118
Bathyllus, 75
Becker, C., 55, 61
Bentley, R., 54, 104–19
Bion, 18
Bostock, Ballad of Tom, 117
Brontë, E., 118
Buecheler, F., 8, 116
Büchner, K., 72–4
Bullatius, 65

Caesar Augustus, 20, 23, 33f., 42,
 44, 56f., 64, 78

Calvus, 3
Campbell, A. Y., 22
Canidia, 51
Catalepton, 73
Catiline, 68
Catius, 35f.
Cato (Censor), 11f.
Cato, *see* Valerius Cato
Catullus, 3, 46, 52, 73
Cicero, 1, 17f., 24, 30, 40, 66, 68–
 74, 77
Cinara, 61
Claudius (Emperor), 72
Commager, S., 42
comparatio paratactica, 55
Cornelius Nepos, 74
Courbaud, E., 42, 52, 55, 61, 66
Crispinus, 41

Damasippus, 39, 75
Davies, J., 105
Davus, 40–2, 63
Dilke, O. A. W., 66
Dio Cassius, 74
Diogenes, 60

Ellis, R., 107
Ennius, 10, 26, 30, 76f., 115
envy (*invidia*), Horace's preoccupa-
 tion with, 16, 33, 39, 51, 56, 78
Epicurus, 47, 52, 63f.

[1] Selective. Does not cover 'Bibliographical Note' and Appendix I ('Horatiana').

2. Passages discussed

HORACE

MACROBIUS

OVID

PLINY

University of Pennsylvania Libraries
www.library.upenn.edu
Circulation Department
vpcircdk@pobox.upenn.edu / 215-898-7556

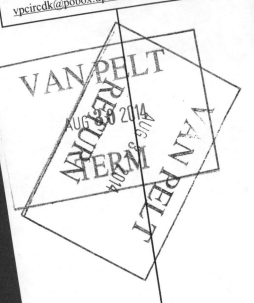

VAN PELT
RETURN
TERM
AUG 30 2014
VAN PELT